Kashmir Shaivism

SUNY Series in Cultural Perspectives
Antonio T. de Nicolas, Editor

Kashmir Shaivism

J. C. Chatterji

State University of New York Press

Published by
State University of New York Press, Albany

Printed in the United States of America

For information, address State University of New York
Press, State University Plaza, Albany, N.Y., 12246

Library of Congress Cataloging-in-Publication Data

Chatterji, Jagadish Chandra.
Kashmir Shaivism.

Reprint. Originally published: Srinagar : Research
Department, Kashmir State, 1914.
Includes index.
1. Kashmir Shaivism. I. Title.
BL1281.154.C43 1986 294.5'513'0954913 85-30365
ISBN 0-88706-179-6
ISBN 0-88706-180-X (pbk.)

Contents

Preface

What is Kashmir Shaivism? A simple answer would be to say that Kashmir Shaivism is a philosophical, religious tradition that seems to have had its genesis in northern India between the eighth and twelfth centuries AD. In it we find a complete system that addresses with remarkable vision the age-old questions, "Who am I? Why am I here? What is the purpose of life? How was this universe created? How should I live my life?" This complex, multi-faceted tradition speaks with equal authority and clarity to Western philosophers and Eastern mystics.

Perhaps this is to be expected, for Kashmir Shaivism emerged at a time when various philosophical and religious schools of thought were engaged in active hermeneutic exchange. Kashmir Shaivism responded to this situation by generating within itself a fusion of apparently contradictory concepts. This does not mean that Kashmir Shaivism arose as a result of facile eclecticism. It did not take a little Advaita Vedanta, add some Madhyamaka Buddhism, and spice it with some yogic practices. Kashmir Shaivism is a complete and coherent system, which according to its own tradition, was revealed by Divine inspiration.

However, it is also true that after the initial revelation was given to Vasagupta, the sages of Kashmir Shaivism were continually in communication with Advaita Vedantins, Buddhists, Grammarians, and Logicians. In the process of this dialogue, Kashmir Shaivism managed to maintain the integrity and consistency of its original revelation, while absorbing several of the primary ideas of each of the other traditions. In this sense, Kashmir Shaivism has been synthetic and creative.

The essential orientation of Kashmir Shaivism is this two-fold movement of embracing change, but within the context of a transcendent truth. Kashmir Shaivism, like many Buddhist schools, acknowledges that this world of ceaseless change is empirically real, and yet unlike Buddhism, bases that reality on a transcendent Consciousness that is simultaneously static and dynamic, that is above these categories and yet also their foundation.

Kashmir Shaivism has many different names for this Consciousness, one of the most frequent being *Parama Shiva.* The ontological nature of *Parama Shiva* is beyond human knowledge and articulation, yet it can be experienced directly through mystical intuition. *Parama Shiva's* nature is limitless, unfathomable, yet as the transcendent subject, it is, itself, the ultimate source for all knowledge. In *Parama Shiva,* we find a fixed, immovable Consciousness that is ever-renewed, ever young, a Consciousness that is simultaneously *Shiva* and *Shakti,* static and dynamic, male and female, potentiality and creativity, transcendent and immanent, beyond expression, yet given form in words.

Kashmir Shaivism is primarily soteriological. It can be studied as an abstract philosophical system, as an objective body of knowledge to be examined at a discrete academic distance, but the real knowledge that Kashmir Shaivism has to offer arises from the practice of the Yoga of Kashmir Shaivism.

Historically, this practice took place within the context of the master/disciple relationship. All of the great teachers of Kashmir Shaivism were themselves disciples. The knowledge that they taught was learned in the context of this relationship. This knowledge arises from active participation in the rigorous experiential process initiated by an enlightened master.

While not everyone, especially in the modern world, is able or willing to enter into a relationship with Kashmir

Shaivism as vivid and demanding as that between student and spiritual master, it is important to remember that this relationship was the context in which Kashmir Shaivism was created and sustained. It was meant to be applied. There is an eminently practical, earthy quality to the philosophy; it is a mysticism of common sense. The most abstract concepts taught by Kashmir Shaivism are based not only on logical thoroughness and mystical insights, but also on a study of the microcosm and ordinary experience. Kashmir Shaivism teaches the essential identity of the Self, God, and the world. The Yoga allows for everything in life to be a contact point with Divinity, a springboard into an experience of transcendence. Riding a horse, listening to a piece of beautiful music, or even simply going to sleep at night can all become the basis for an encounter with Divinity if seen with the correct understanding.

Kashmir Shaivism accepts the reality of the world as it is, with all its happiness and pain, and beauty and ugliness. It views the world not as an illusion, but as the creative manifestation of *Parama Shiva*. The entire universe comes forth out of the *Svatantrya* or perfect freedom of the Lord. The world is a joyful expression of the *Shakti*, the power or Consciousness of *Parama Shiva*. Out of Herself and because of Herself, this consciousness eternally projects the world, unfolding the world upon Herself as upon a screen. All forms of artistic expression whether dance, poetry, drama, or music were created by *Shiva* and *Shakti*. If understood correctly, every moment of life can be an occasion for coming into contact with the artist of creation—can be a way to touch that source of joy and ecstasy that underlies the entire universe.

This perception enables seekers to pierce through the surface to previously unperceived layers of meaning, and to alter radically how they interact with other human beings. With this changed vision, they can sense the interconnections that link everything in the world, and can directly experience that each action they perform resonates throughout the entire universe. As they assimilate the knowledge offered by Kashmir Shaivism into their being, they begin to realize their own worth and significance. They see that as inner worlds open up inside, the outer world also tends to reflect that change; they see that as joy is discovered inside, the outer world also appears more joyous. According to Kashmir Shaivism, the world is a mirror through which a person can gain self-knowledge in their interaction with others. They continually discover their own face in the world and find their own meaning in life reflected back to them. They also ultimately discover that the face in the mirror of the world is the face of God, that the shining presence of Divinity pervades their entire being and speaks to them through the sounds and colors of the world.

Kashmir Shaivism often separates God's creative activity into two distinct categories: involution and evolution. Involution, the arch of descent, is the manifestation of the universe in which *Shakti* purposefully conceals Herself in the act of creation, forgetting Her true nature. Evolution, the arch of ascent, is the process of discovery through which *Shakti*, reduced now to limited human awareness, recognizes the world as not separate from Herself, and begins once again to enjoy Her true nature as supremely free and joyous Consciousness.

J.C. Chatterji's *Kashmir Shaivism* focuses primarily on the movement of descent, in great detail describing the cosmological process of involution. Each of the *tattvas*, or levels of manifestation, is pictured in such a way that even the most abstract and subtle steps of the process can be clearly understood. Chatterji, true to the Kashmir Shaivite tradition, draws upon everyday life to illustrate lucidly how every person continually experiences each of the *tattvas*. Chatterji mentions that he also intends to give a brief account of the process of evolution; unfortunately, he never finished that section of the book. It is important to understand that the *tattvas* are not only stages of manifestion, descriptions of the process through which

Consciousness becomes the world and the human soul, they are also a ladder of ascent, a diagram of different levels of mystical awareness. The philosopher-mystics of Kashmir Shaivism described the *tattvas* not only as cosmological categories, but as points of reference that a person involved in the spiritual journey could directly experience in super-conscious states of awareness.

According to Kashmir Shaivism, the evolutionary movement of a human being begins with *anugraha*, the bestowal of divine grace. Supreme Consciousness, contracted into the form of human awareness, has become so bound up in the world, so alienated from its true glory, that it needs to be awakened from this sleep of self-imposed ignorance and reminded of its true nature as Supreme Consciousness. This moment of awakening, this recognition of Self-Divinity, is *anugraha*, and in a very real sense, the Divine bestows this grace upon itself. This Self-bestowal of grace is possible only because Consciousness always remains transcendent, even while immersed in the world of separation and change.

This *anugraha* is also called *shakti-pata*, or the descent of Divine power. *Shakti-pata* is the *diksha*, or initiation, that enables a human being to begin the pursuit of Self-knowledge ultimately culminating in a complete and perfect reunion with *Parama Shiva*. According to Kashmir Shaivism, this dispensation of grace rarely descends directly from the Lord, but usually occurs through the vehicle of a spiritual master who is fully awakened to his or her own divinity. The spiritual master is thus seen as indispensable for the process of evolution. He or she not only teaches and guides the disciple, but also acts as the initial catalyst that kindles the disciple's latent potential.

Obviously, not everyone is involved with the arch of ascent, and even among those who are, there are vast differences in temperament and spiritual receptivity. Although Kashmir Shaivism teaches that all human beings are fundamentally equal, that everyone is a manifestation of the same divine Consciousness, at the same time, it is a preeminently practical system. Kashmir Shaivism recognizes that each person is unique, and will approach the task of gaining self-knowledge in different ways.

In order to be appropriate to particular individuals, Kashmir Shaivism has inherent within its system four different levels of spiritual practice called *upayas*, or means. The divisions between these *upayas* are not impermeable and quite often one person will use techniques from each level. However, each *upaya* has certain characteristics by which it can be identified.

The foundational *upaya* is called *Anava upaya*, or the path of the *anu*, the "point", or individual soul. This *upaya* has to do with practices performed by persons who feel separate from God, and want to perform actions with their body and senses in order to purify themselves. Typical spiritual techniques often included in this *upaya* are chanting, hatha yoga postures, breathing practices, mechanical repetition of a mantra, or meditation on an image of God.

The next *upaya* is *Shakta upaya*, the spiritual practices that focus on the various manifestations and activity of the *Shakti*, or divine power. *Shakta upaya* is the path of realization through knowledge. This *upaya* is designed for those who possess primarily a dual/non-dual awareness. It is for people who have an intellectual understanding of the teachings of Kashmir Shaivism, yet who are unable to hold this awareness and actualize it in their daily lives. In *Shakta upaya* comprises a series of techniques designed to reorient a person in the direction of divinity, that help to overcome the innate tendency to feel small, powerless, and cut off both from the Lord and other people.

There are countless techniques included in *Shakta upaya*. One of the most basic is the investigation of the mantra. Instead of a mechanical repetition, as in *anava upaya*, this technique asks the person to view the mantra, not as a mere collection of letters, but as a pulsation of consciousness, throbbing Shakti that has the power, if correctly understood, to carry awareness back to its source, Pure Consciousness. In this practice, the person repeats the mantra with the realization that the mantra, the deity the mantra refers to, and his or her own being are identical, that they are all forms of one Consciousness.

A person can also meditate on the true nature of the mind and become aware that his or her thoughts are nothing but different forms of Consciousness. With this awareness, one might then simply observe thoughts as they arise and subside, subtly trace those thoughts back to their source, and grasp that moment of stillness between the thoughts, the *unmesha*, the reservoir of Divine potency.

Gaining access to the *unmesha* can be accomplished in many different ways, but it always seems that it is found in the world of the in-between, in the moment between waking and sleep, in the space between the breaths, even between moments of perception. *Unmesha* is the unseen, normally unfelt backdrop of existence, the ocean of awareness and potentiality from which each of the countless waves of consciousness arise and subside. It can be touched at any moment, but is normally revealed only to the probing of a subtle and refined intellect.

In reality, *Shakta upaya* is not so much a series of techniques, but a reorientation to life, a particular way of understanding and relating to the world and oneself. *shakta upaya* is a type of self-directed mental reprogramming where a person counterbalances the negative, limited concepts of him or herself and the world with new patterns of understanding. In *Shakta upaya*, a person consciously reflects on the teachings of Kashmir Shaivism, and puts them into practice through creative contemplation. For instance, a person might tell him or herself, "I am Shiva, I am the Lord, I pervade everywhere, this entire universe is nothing but the reflection of my own glory," and eventually, because these statements represent ontological truths, they set up a particular resonance inside the disciple that responds to those truths. What was previously only an abstract mental formulation then moves to a deeper, more experiential level, and the disciple begins to merge with the particular inner state of consciousness.

This deeper, nonmental stage of practice is the key to the third *upaya, Shambava upaya*, the path of identification with *shambhava*, or *shiva*. In *Shambhava upaya*, no actions or even thoughts are involved. The person, having saturated his or her being with repeated thoughts of the Divine, now lets go and rests in the awareness of the essential Self, with just a subtle effort of will. In the first two *upayas*, the person was like an archer who places the arrow on the string, pulls the bow taut and aims for the target. But in order for the arrow to be able to plunge into the target, the archer has to let go. This letting go is *Shambhava upaya*. Here seekers practice "alert passivity" or "choiceless awareness". They are aware that there really are no practices that can be done to attain that which has always been their own; the person is aware that no techniques can reveal that which surrounds and penetrates his or her very being. In this *upaya*, direct intuitive knowledge of Self flashes forth of its own accord.

Shambhava upaya, at its highest maturity, culminates in the final *upaya, Anupaya*, which means "little or no effort." *Anupaya* is simple, direct, complete Recognition or *Pratyabhijna*. With just one word or one look from the master, or with a spontaneous descent of grace, the person realizes his or her true nature fully and completely. Regardless of what actions may be performed in the world, he or she participates in a state of consciousness that never wavers; he or she effortlessly and naturally remains absorbed in the highest Reality, and revels in the joy of his or her own Being.

We have in Kashmir Shaivism both a sophisticated philosophy and a practical mode of interacting with the world suited to our modern era.

William Barnard
Temple University

Foreword

Interest in Kashmir Shaivism among scholars begins in the middle of the last century and has continued slowly until our day. The attraction that Shaivism has for us comes in part from its findings about the origin and nature of the universe, which so closely approximate the conclusions of our contemporary scientists that they appear astonishingly modern.

More than a philosophy, Shaivism is a way of experiencing life. Because of its ample vision as well as the depth of its understanding of the human being, Shaivism has been conquering the hearts of people in all parts of the world. It was the late Swami Muktananda Paramahansa (1908-1982) who made Shaivism popular in the West through his lectures and books. Wherever Swami Muktananda traveled, whether in the United States, Europe or Australia, he used the teachings of Shaivism to help people open to the understanding of life as a divine experience.

Shiva, the deity of Shaivism, is of the nature of *Chidānanda*, Consciousness and bliss. The essential message of Shaivism is the vision that the world and our life are manifestations of the play of divine Consciousness. In the words of Swami Muktananda: "The truth is that to realize the Self is to get what we already have. There is nothing apart from Shiva. There is nothing other than Shiva. Whatever there is is Shiva. To be aware of Parashiva is to be fearless and free in the Self. There is nothing which is not Shiva, there is no place which is not Shiva. Not a single thought wave can arise separate from Shiva. To be aware of this is to be aware of Shiva." All of

Shaivism's concern is thus completely focused in offering a means to uplift the condition of human beings and return the experience of happiness that is theirs by birthright.

In this book we deal with the *Pratyabhijnā Darshana.* The term "Kashmir Shaivism," though popular, is not very accurate since in Kashmir there was more than one form of Shaivism. The Shaivism of Kashmir included the philosophic schools of Trika, Kaula and Krama, not to mention the various manifestations of Shaivite religion itself. A series of great spiritual masters, who lived in that region of North India between the 8th and 11th centuries A.D., developed a branch of the ancient Shaivite tradition into a spiritual philosophy. Vasugupta, Somananda, Utpaladeva and Abhinavagupta were the sages who gave shape to what eventually became known as the *Pratyabhijnā Darshana*, the philosophy of recognition. For them, Shiva is not simply the destructive god and eccentric yogi of the *Purānas*, the texts of Hindu mythology. Shiva is the supreme truth, the eternal Self that abides in all things. This is how the *Shvetāshvatara Upanishad* (3.16) describes it: "With hands and feet, everywhere, everywhere with eye, head and mouth, with ears everywhere, It stands enclosing all in the universe." Shiva is the *ātman*, the inner Self of all sentient and insentient beings.

The enormous advantage a human being has over other creatures is his capacity to see and experience the Truth. This experience is the main theme of the philosophy of recognition. In India, philosophical activity is intimately linked to the mystical experience. The few strictly materialistic or atheist philosophical systems ended relegated to the dust of libraries. Only the classical *darshanas* like Vedanta, Sankhya, Yoga and the Āgamas have remained alive. Philosophy in India is *darshana*, that is, the mystical experience explained through reason. The word *darshana* properly interpreted means "vision"—the vision an individual has of God's manifestation. This is why the classical *darshanas* of Indian philosophy deal with three fundamental themes: the nature of God, the universe and the human being.

The mystic, both man and woman, is someone who practices a series of processes that lead him towards a total fusion with the Truth. These processes are known under the general name of *yoga* because, as the word implies, it is a way to "yoke" the individual with the divine experience. To realize God is to become that Truth oneself. For the yogi to "philosophize" is not only and exclusively to speculate on metaphysics or support his conclusions with the use of logic. *Tarka*, reasoning, is an instrument in the service of the mystical experience. It serves as a means to put the ineffable into words, so that the mind can understand it better.

Pratyabhijnā, as understood by the Kashmiri sages, is the direct recognition that Shiva, the supreme Self, is our most intimate inner Self. Literally translated, *Pratyabhijnā* means "recognition", that is, to know again something we already knew. It is a paradoxical experience from the point of view of common sense: How can we re-cognize something we already know? Shaivism explains that through a cosmic act of Shiva we forgot we are Shiva and through another act of Shiva we receive the grace that removes this ignorance so we know again who in reality we are. For the sages of the *Pratyabhijnā* the Self is that which never changes, never has changed and never will change. The Self is *Chidānanda*, sovereign and free Consciousness and eternal joy.

According to Shaivism, there cannot be full recognition without divine grace. The sages of Kashmir called *shaktipāta* the descent of Shiva's grace on those seekers who wanted to know the Truth. *Shaktipāta* is the cornerstone of the entire philosophy and yoga of *Pratyabhijnā*, as it is the means by which the individual is saved from the pains of his limited condition and recovers the plenitude of *Chidānanda*, the bliss of divine Consciousness.

A seeker can obtain *shaktipāta* directly from the Supreme Being if he has accumulated immense merit in the course of many lives dedicated to devotion to the Lord and uplifting his soul through spiritual practices. But this way of attaining grace is uncertain as well as slow. The majority of seekers resort to the easiest means, that is to put themselves at the service of a Guru with the power of giving *shaktipāta.* In his commentary to the *Shiva Sūtras* (II, 6), Kshemaraja defines the God-realized Guru as one with Shiva and therefore a vehicle for Shiva's grace to flow in the world: *Guruvā pārameshvarī anugrahikā shaktih*—"The Guru is the grace bestowing power of the Lord."

Under the Guru's guidance, the seeker voluntarily submits himself to the process of *yoga* to purify his system from those impediments that prevent him from recognizing the Self. Shaivism groups these impediments under the heading of three basic impurities called *malas. Ānava mala* is the impurity that makes us feel imperfect and disconnected from God. *Māyīya mala* is the impurity of duality that makes us perceive each other as different and separated from the rest of creation. *Kārma mala* is the impurity that reduces our activity to limited actions and makes us suffer the destiny of transmigration. The *malas* contract the innate liberty and plenitude of Shiva to convert him into a human being. This process occurs because Shiva desires it; it is an act of Shiva's free will.

"Why are we condemned to suffer the ups and downs of this world? Why can't we enjoy Shiva's eternal ecstasy?" This perennial question the Shaivite sage considers superfluous—like asking why is water wet, or why does fire burn. God's nature is freedom and in his freedom he chooses to hide himself, become a human being (and everything created) and enjoy and suffer his own creation. Therefore, the appropriate question for a spiritual seeker is, "How can I get rid of my suffering and enjoy the pristine condition of Shivahood?"

The philosophy of *Pratyabhijnā* is an attempt to correct the limited condition of the human being. When a seeker receives grace through a Guru, his *Kundalinī* energy is awakened. *Kundalinī* is nothing else but Shiva's own grace working within an individual to purify him. Shaivism adopts the tradition of *Kundalinī Yoga* from the āgamas and tantras. But it is not enough to have received the initiation of *Kundalinī* awakening, the seeker must cooperate with this energy by performing spiritual practices. Yoga and grace go hand-in-hand in this process.

The spiritual practices of Shaivism have a flavor of their own and are quite typical of this system. They are known as *upāyas*, ways or paths. In themselves they are a compilation of yogic techniques taken from the āgamas, Patanjali's yoga, the Upanishads and other traditions and adapted to Shaivism. The most elementary path is *ānavopāya*, which comprises the practices intended to purify the physical and subtle bodies and the mind. This is the path for people who feel separated from the goal of their practices, who feel that the Self or God is other than themselves, for this reason *ānavopāya* is called the dualistic path. Examples of *ānavopāya* are meditation on a deity's form or the repetition of a mantra.

When the seeker has been able to overcome, at least partially, the feeling of duality he automatically enters *shāktopāya*. The essential technique of this path is the mental contemplation of the Self. Instead of repeating a mantra, like *Shivo'ham* (I am Shiva), the meditator contemplates the fundamental experience communicated by the mantra. He tries to maintain a witnessing awareness of the divine presence within himself. The mind still operates as an entity separate from the Self but on its way to merging in the experience of Shiva. For this reason *shāktopāya* is dualist and nondualist at the same time. With practice, the separation between the mind and the Self gradually dissolves until the seeker imperceptibly flows into the next path.

In *shāmbhavopāya* the seeker does not have to make any personal efforts. The *icchā shakti*, Shiva's will power, takes care of eliminating all residue of impurity so that the seeker attains divine realization. *Shāmbhavopāya* is essentially the path of nonduality.

The sage Abhinavagupta used to explain that when the seeker becomes anchored in his experience of *shāmbhavopāya* he is flooded by a state of plenitude called *anupāya*, the path without practices, the techniqueless technique. *Anupāya* is the culmination of *shāmbhavopāya*, when the seeker experiences a total and permanent recognition of his Self. The sages of Kashmir were fond of claiming that *anupāya* is the exclusive characteristic of the yogic process of *Pratyabhijnā Darshana*.

The final experience does not annihilate the existence of the world for the mystic. The mystic does not become "mystical", ethereal and disconnected from life. On the contrary, for the mystic, life acquires an exalted feeling. This state is described in the *Shiva Sūtras* (I, 18) as: *Lokānanda samādhi sukham*—"The ecstasy of the world is the bliss of *samādhi*." The *samādhi* of Shaivism is not only an internal experience of meditation, but encompasses all of Shiva's creation. Swami Chidvilasananda, who continues the work of Swami Muktananda, describes the state of a realized being in this way: "Such a person doesn't shrink from the world, he accepts the world as it comes. We think that on the spiritual path we accept what is good and reject what is bad, but in this way we alienate ourselves from the world. A true devotee of God accepts the world as it is and by the power of his love transforms it. As long as we reject the world, the world will reject us. When you love the world as God, the world loves you and gives you its grace." Shaivism does not consider the world unreal. When we recognize our inner Self as Shiva and the world as Shiva we stop feeling alienated from the world around us and life becomes a constant participation in Shiva's ecstatic play.

But let us return to the book and its author. It was J.C. Chatterji who made the major initial effort of bringing into the public light the fascinating unfoldment of Kashmir's Shaivite philosophy. He was the first director of the Kashmir Research Department, a center for philosophic and historical investigations established by one of the maharajas of Kashmir in the 1850's. Though the center had been founded years before, it did not start functioning effectively until 1902. Under Chatterji's inspired direction, the center began, in 1904, to edit and publish manuscripts on Shaivism. Many of these manuscripts were still in the hands of the families of Kashmiri pandits who had kept them as heirlooms for generations. The Kashmir Research Department continued this labor in subsequent years to include almost all the known texts on *Pratyabhijnā*.

Kashmir Shaivaism (sic) was part of this series of publications and a pioneering book. When it first appeared in 1914 there was very little information about Shaivism. Chatterji's intention was to give a general idea of *Pratyabhijnā's* main themes. Unfortunately, Chatterji never concluded his original project. The explanation on the *upāyas* and the planned appendixes are missing. He also failed to write about some key themes of Shaivism like *shaktipāta*, the *malas*, the origin of ignorance and the realization of God, among others. Nonetheless, it is to the credit of the author's scholarship that the most recent investigations have not modified significantly his observations on *Pratyabhijnā's* historical development. His explanation on the *tattvas*, the cosmic principles of the creative process, continues to be the standard in the field. To understand the *tattvas* in Shaivism is as important as learning the alphabet is in studying a language, for the *tattvas* are the skeleton upon which is mounted the entire thought and the mystic experience of Shaivism. Chatterji was also the first to make the distinction between the revealed texts, the ones that simply state the themes of Shaivism, and those texts that rationalize the themes.

Perhaps following a custom of the 19th century, he classifies as "religious" the first period of *Pratyabhijnā's* development, meaning that its texts act as articles of faith. That is the period of Vasugupta, Kallata, the *Shiva Sūtras* and the *Spanda Kārikās.* The works he calls "philosophic" belong to the following generations, of Somananda, Utpaladeva, Abhinavagupta and Kshemaraja, in which the Shaivite thought is elaborated and expanded with the use of logical reasoning. Chatterji's book, even though it remains unfinished, still continues to be one of the best introductions to Kashmir Shaivism that we have at hand.

Swami Shantananda
South Fallsburg, New York

PART I

The Main Doctrines of the System

Having thus glanced at its history and literature, let us now consider briefly the main doctrines of the Trika or Advaita Shaiva Philosophy of Kashmir. I propose to state these clearly but briefly, *without entering into an exposition of the reasonings*[1] which are, or can be, adduced in their support; for such a task would obviously be impossible in what is intended to be but a short introduction to the study of the subject. We may perhaps begin by enunciating the view the Trika holds of the true and ultimate nature of an experiencing being. It may be stated as follows[2] :—

THE ĀTMAN

The Ātman, that is the true and innermost Self in every being, is a changeless reality of the nature of a purely experiencing principle,[3] as distinguished from whatever may *assume the form*[4] of either the experienced or of the means of experience.

1. For the reasonings in support of some of the doctrines which the Trika holds in common with the other systems of Indian Philosophy, see *Hindu Realism* by the author.

2. All that is said in the following paragraphs is based on the texts as given in Appendix I.

3. चैतन्यमात्मा; *Shiv. Sū.*, i. 1.

4. There is in reality neither any experienced nor means of experience which, in its essence, is other than the

6

It is called Chaitanya[1] and also Parā Saṁvit, the Supreme Experience; Parameshvara, the Supreme Lord; Shiva, the Benign One; or Parama Shiva,[2] the Supreme Shiva. These two last names are what I shall chiefly use here, and shall therefore refer to this principle in the masculine as He, even though in reality it is neither He, She nor It, and may be equally referred to by any or all of these terms.

It is impossible to render Chaitanya or Chit in English by any single word which would adequately convey all that is implied by this technical term. We must therefore retain it untranslated.

This Chaitanya or Parama Shiva is the Reality which underlies, as its innermost and true self, not only every experiencing being but also every thing else in the universe, both separately, *i. e.*, individually, as well as a totality, *i. e.*, as the entire universe as a whole.

As the underlying reality in every thing and being in the universe, Parama Shiva is one and the same in them all—undivided and unlimited by any of them, however much they may be separated either in time or in space. In other words, Parama Shiva is beyond the limits of time, space and form; and as such is Eternal and Infinite.

Again, as the underlying reality in everything, He is all-pervading; and *at the same time* He is also all transcending. That is to say, His nature has primarily a two-

---

Experiencer. It is the Experiencer itself that assumes the form of the experienced. इह हि सर्वत्र अप्रतिहतशक्तिः परमेश्वर एव तथाबुभूषुस्तथाभवति; न तु अन्यः कश्चित् परमार्थतः अस्ति इति असकृदुक्तम् ॥ *Pra. Vi.*, I. i. 7.

1. Or simply Chit. But as this word is also used to signify an aspect of Shakti, we may, to avoid confusion, reserve it exclusively for that use. See below pp. 43, 44.

2. The name Parama Shiva would seem to be a later one, but the fact has always been recognised. See *Shiva Dṛiṣh.*, i. 2.

fold aspect—an immanent aspect in which He pervades the universe, and a transcendental aspect in which He is beyond all Universal Manifestations.

Indeed, the Universe with all its infinite variety of objects, and means, of experience is nothing but a manifestation of the immanent aspect of Parama Shiva himself. It has no other basis or ingredient in it.[1]

This aspect of His is called Shakti (Power), which, being only an aspect, is not in any way different from, or independent of, Parama Shiva, but is one and the same with Him.[2] If anything, it is His creative Power, and is spoken of as His feminine aspect, as will be done here also.

Shakti again has several, indeed an infinite number of, aspects or modes, of which five are the most fundamental and primary ones.[3] These are:

i. The Power of Self-Revelation whereby Shiva—as

---

1. श्रीमत्परमशिवस्य पुनः विश्वोत्तीर्ण–विश्वात्मक–परमानन्दमय-प्रकाशैकघनस्य... अखिलम् अभेदेनैव स्फुरति; न तु वस्तुतः अन्यत् किञ्चित् ग्राह्यं ग्राहकं वा; अपि तु श्रीपरमशिवभट्टारक एव इत्थं नानावैचित्र्यसहस्रैः स्फुरति ।

Pra. Hṛid., p. 8.

चिदेव भगवती.........तत्तदनन्तजगदात्मना स्फुरति ।

Ibid., p. 3.

आत्मैव सर्वभावेषु स्फुरन्निर्वृतचिद्विभुः ।
अनिरुद्धेच्छाप्रसरः प्रसरद्दृक्–क्रियः शिवः ॥ *Shiv. Dṛiṣh.*, i. 2.

2. पराशक्तिरूपा चितिरेव भगवती...शिवभट्टारकाभिन्ना ।; *Prat. Hṛid.*, p. 2.
न शिवः शक्तिरहितो न शक्तिर्व्यतिरेकिणी ।
शिवः शक्तस्तथा भावान् इच्छया कर्तुमीहते ।
शक्ति-शक्तिमतोर्भेदः शैवे जातु न वर्ण्यते ॥ *Shiv. Dṛiṣh.*, iii. 2, 3.

3. शक्तयश्च असंख्येयाः । *Tan. Sār.*, Āhn. iv.

मुख्याभिः (पञ्चभिः) शक्तिभिर्युक्तः । *Ibid.*, Āhn. i.

परमेश्वरः पञ्चभिः शक्तिभिर्निर्भरः' । *Ibid.*, Āhn. ii.

The five aspects even are reduced to but three: इत्येवं मुख्याभिः [पञ्चभिः] शक्तिभिर्युक्तोऽपि वस्तुतः इच्छा-ज्ञान-क्रियाशक्तियुक्तः......शिवरूपः । *Tantrasāra*, Āhn. i.

Parama Shiva in reference to this aspect of Shakti is called—shines as it were by himself, even when there is nothing objective to reveal or shine upon, like the sun in the material world as it would be if it could be conceived as shining all by itself, even when there was no object which it might light up or of which it might reveal the existence. It is the *Chit-Shakti* of the Supreme Lord (*lit.* the Power of Intelligence or the pure Light of Intelligence by itself).[1]

ii. The Power of realising absolute Bliss and Joy, which is ever satisfied in itself without there ever being any need for an object or means, and without ever going or *moving* out of itself for its satisfaction, and which is therefore ever *independent* and free and is ever *at rest,* as an ever undisturbed peace.

This is the Ānanda Shakti of Parama Shiva (*lit.* the Power of Joying).[2]

iii. The Power of feeling oneself as supremely able and of an absolutely irresistible Will,—the Power also of what may be called the feeling of 'divine wonder' and of forming a divine Resolve as to what to do or create.

This is the Ichchhā Shakti of Parama Shiva (lit. the Will Power.)[3]

---

1. प्रकाशरूपता चिच्छक्तिः । *Tan. Sār.*, Āhn. i.
प्रकाशश्च अनन्योन्मुखविमर्शः अहमिति । *Pra. Vi.*, III. i. 4.

2. स्वातन्त्र्यम् आनन्दशक्तिः । *Tan. Sār.*, Āhn. i.
आनन्दः स्वातन्त्र्यम्, स्वात्मविश्रान्तिस्वभावाह्लादप्राधान्यात् । *Tan. Sār.*
स्वतन्त्रश्च पुनः "यो हि तथाबुभूषुः न प्रतिहन्यते सः" ।
Pra. Vi. Vi., fol. 258.

3. तच्चमत्कार इच्छाशक्तिः ॥ *Tan. Sār.*, Āhn. i.
तथाबुभूषालक्षणा । *Pra. Vi. Vi.*, fol. 258.
इच्छाया हि ज्ञानक्रिययोः साम्यरूपाभ्युपगमात्मकत्वात् ॥
Tan. Sār., Āhn. 2.
And therefore चमत्कारः, that is, as it were न ययौ न तस्थौ ।

iv. The Power of bringing and holding all objects in conscious relations with oneself and also with one another.

This is the Jñāna Shakti (lit. the Power of Knowledge or Knowing, of Consciousness pure and simple without any reference to emotional Feeling or Will).[1]

v. The Power of assuming any and every form *i. e.* Creating, which, as will be seen, has no other meaning.

This is the Kriyā Shakti of the Supreme Shiva.[2]

With these five principal aspects of his Shakti, of which there are in reality, as said above, an infinite number of modes, Parama Shiva manifests himself—or which is the same thing he manifests his Shakti—as the Universe. And he does this of his own free and independent will (svechchhayā) without the use of any other material save his own Power, and in Himself as the basis of the Universe. (svabhittau).[3]

Thus, in reality, the Universe is only an "expansion" of the Power of Parama Shiva Himself; or—to put it perhaps more correctly—of Parama Shiva in his aspect as Shakti,[4] by which aspect he both becomes and pervades the Universe thus produced, while yet He remains the ever transcendent Chaitanya without in any way whatsoever being affected by the manifestation of a Universe.[5]

---

1. आमर्षात्मकता ज्ञानशक्तिः । *Tan. Sār.*, Ahn. i. आमर्ष is again defined as ईषत्तया वेद्योन्मुखता, *i. e.*, just the awareness of the object as a mere presentation without any feeling or action of going out toward it—without reacting.

2. सर्वाकारयोगित्वं क्रियाशक्तिः । *Ibid.*.

3. *Pra. Hṛid.*, Sū. 2.

4. स्वशक्तिप्रचयोऽस्य विश्वम् ॥ *Shiv. Sū.*, iii. 30.

अनिरुद्धेच्छाप्रसरः प्रसरद्दृक्-क्रियः शिवः । *Shiv. Dṛiṣh.*, i. 2.

5. A friendly European critic has characterised this statement as only an expression of theological prejudice. See however note given in Appendix II.

When Shakti expands or opens herself out (unmiṣhati), the Universe comes to be, and when She gathers or closes herself up (nimiṣhati)[1], the Universe disappears as a manifestation, *i. e.* as 'predicable' in terms of discursive thought and speech (vāchya).[2]

But it is not once only that She thus opens herself out, or that She will gather herself up; nor is the present Universe the first and only one which has come into manifestation. On the contrary, there have been countless Universes before and there will be an equally countless number of them in the endless futurity of time—the Universes, thus produced, following one another and forming a series in which they are linked together by the relation of causal necessity; that is to say, each successive Universe coming into existence as an inevitable consequence of certain causes (to be explained later) generated in the one preceding it.

Thus it happens, that, instead of the Divine Shakti opening herself out and gathering herself up only once, she has gone on repeating the process eternally, there being to it neither an absolute beginning nor a final ending. In other words, She alternates herself eternally between a phase of manifestation or explication and a phase of potentiality, bringing a universe into existence

1. *Pra. Hṛid.*, p. 2.; also *Spa. Kā.* 1.

2. On the Vāchyatva of the universe and its existence in a non-Vāchya form prior to manifestation, compare, among others, the following passages:—

गर्भीकृतानन्तविश्व इति क्रोडीकृतनिखिल-वाच्यवाचककलापः ।

Tantrāl. Viv., Āhn. iii.

वाच्यवाचकात्मनि विश्वत्र । *Ibid.*

यन्माहात्म्यान् निखिलोऽयं वाच्य-वाचकात्मा सृष्ट्यवभासः स्यात् । *Ibid.*

अशेषवाच्य-वाचकमयं जगत् । *Vijñā. Bhai. Ud.*

शून्यादि-क्षित्यन्तमनन्तं वाच्यवाचकरूपम् । *Ibid.*

भुवनादित्रयं वाच्यं पदादिवाचकं त्रयम् ।

शक्तिरेतच्चाध्वषट्कं शक्तिमांस्तु महेश्वरः ॥ *Ibid.*

when she assumes the manifesting phase, and reducing it to what may be called a seminal state or form, when she passes into the potential phase.

Such a phase of manifestation or actuality of the Shakti is called an Udaya, Unmeṣha, Ābhāsana (lit. an appearance, a shining forth) or Sṛiṣhṭi, while a potential phase is termed a Pralaya (dissolution); and a complete cycle consisting of a Sṛiṣhṭi and a Pralaya (a creation and a dissolution) is technically named a Kalpa (lit. an 'imagining' 'assuming' or 'ideating,' namely, of a creation and a dissolution).[1]

Now, even though of an infinite variety, the things and beings, of which the Universe, thus produced by the 'opening out' of Shakti, consists, are built up really of only a few fundamental and general factors technically called the Tattvas, (lit. the thatness or whatness[2], namely, of everything that exists). What these really are will be made clear as we go on. In the meantime they may be just enumerated here for the purpose of convenient reference.

Counting from what is, as it were, farthest removed from the ultimate Reality, that is to say, in which the

---

1. For the use of these terms in the above senses, see, among others, *Spa. Kā.*, 1; *Pra. Hṛid.*, Sū. 11; &c. Comp. also the Vedic passage, यथापूर्वमकल्पयत् *Ṛeg. V.*, X. 190. 3.

अस्यां हि चिति प्रसरन्त्यां जगदुन्मिषति...निवृत्तप्रसरायां च निमिषति । *Pra. Hṛid.*, p. 2.

For some of the reasons in support of the doctrine of 'Kalpa' see my *Hindu Realism*, pp. 95–100, 125–128. संहार means 'बीजावस्थापन' with a view to *re*manifestation. See, among others, *Pra. Hṛid.*, Sū. 11 and Comment. on it (pp. 24 &c.).

2. तस्य भावस्तत्त्वमिति भिन्नानां वर्गाणां वर्गीकरणनिमित्तं यदेकमविभक्तं भाति तत् तत्त्वम्, यथा गिरिवृक्षपुरप्रभृतीनां नदीसरःसागरादीनां च पृथिवीरूपत्वम् अब्-रूपत्वं चेति; *Pra. Vi.*, III. i. 2.

nature of the Reality is the most veiled, the Tattvas may be enumerated as follows[1]:—

I. Five Factors constituting what may be termed the materiality of the sensible universe *viz:*

1. The principle of Solidity or Stability, technically called the Pṛithivī or Dharā-Tattva; lit. Earth.
2. The principle of Liquidity—technically Ap; lit. Water.
3. The principle of what may be called Formativity *i. e.* the Formative or Form building principle—technically Agni; lit. Fire.
4. The principle of Aeriality—technically Vāyu; lit. Air or the aerial atmosphere.
5. The principle of Vacuity (Avakāsha)—technically Ākāsha; Lit. the Sky, the bright shining Firmament.

The above five form a group and are collectively termed the five Bhūtas—lit. things that have *been*, not *are*. We may call them the physical or the sensible group.

II. Five Principles constituting what become the powers of the motor-nervous system when they appear in the body, *viz:*

6. The Power or Capacity of enjoying passively and resting with satisfaction in what is, or is *felt* as, one's own or even oneself, without going or moving out;—the power or capacity of recreation; technically the Upastha, lit. the recreative or generative organ.
7. The Power or Capacity of rejecting or discarding

1. The reasons for the translations, as given here, of the technical names of the Tattvas will be made clear as we go on. The texts supporting this interpretation of the Tattvas are also given below. (See also *Hindu Realism*).

what is not needed or liked in an organic system —technically the Pāyu; lit. the voiding or discarding organ.

8. The Power of Locomotion—technically the Pāda; lit. the feet.

9. The Power of Handling—technically the Hasta, lit. the hand.

10. The Power of Expression or voicing—technically the Vāch or the vocal organ.

These five forming a group, are collectively called the Karmendriyas *i. e.* the Indriyas, Powers or Capacities of action or activity.

III. Five General Elements of sense-perception, *viz:*

11. The sense *object* of Odour-as-such, the Gandha-tanmātra.

12. do do of Flavour-as-such, the Rasa-tanmātra.

13. do do of Colour-as such, the Rupa-tanmātra.

14. do do of Feel-as-such, the Sparsha-tanmātra.

15. do do of Sound-as-such, the Shabda-tanmātra.

These five forming the quintad of the *general* objects of the special senses are collectively called the Tanmātras.

IV. Five Powers of sense perception, *viz.*

16. The Power, Capacity or Sense of Smell (Ghrāṇendriya).

17. do do of Taste (Rasanendriya).

18. do do of Sight (Darshanendriya).

19. do do of Feeling-by-Touch (Sparshendriya)

20. do do of Hearing (Shravaṇendriya)

The above five are collectively called the five Jñānendriyas or Buddhīndriyas *i. e.* Indriyas or Powers of sense-perception, or, as they may be called, with reference to their operation in the physical body, the senses.

V. Three Capacities of mental operation, *viz:*

21. The Capacity of concretion and imagination—the Manas, the ever moving or the ever flowing one.
22. The Capacity of 'self-arrogation' and appropriation—the Ahaṅkāra, that which builds up the personal Ego, the 'I' of every-day life of one as Rāma or Shyāma, as John or Jones.
23. The Capacity of Judgment—the Buddhi.

The above three are collectively called the Antaḥkaraṇa, lit. the 'Inner Organ.'

VI. Two principles of the *limited individual* subject-object, *viz*:

24. The Root of all Feeling, that is, Affection in the widest sense of the term; or the Principle of the Affective in general, affecting the experiencer either as (i) the movementless, *i. e.* actionless, and even blissful, Feeling of the *merest presentation* or of pure consciousness or awareness as distinguished from any the slightest moving passion; as (ii) moving Passion in any form or degree; or as (iii) Stupefaction or Dulness in any form or degree;—technically the Prakṛiti, Affecting, or the Affective (lit. the doing forth, She that worketh forth.)
25. That which experiences these in or as a *limited individual* being—technically the Purusha, the Individual.

So far the Tattvas or principles are, as will be seen, the same as those recognised by the Sāṅkhya System of Philosophy, with the only difference that, while the Purusha and the Prakṛiti are the final realities from the Sāṅkhya point of view, they are but derivatives according to the Trika, which, therefore, carrying the analysis further, recognises the following additional Tattvas:—

VII. Six Principles of subjective Limitation, *viz:*

26. (*a*) Limitation in regard to Duration of presence and simultaneity of experience—leading to the necessity of having experiences for limited periods and in succession.—Technically Kāla or Time. (The determinant of 'when').

27. (*b*) Limitation in regard to presence, as in space, *i. e.*, access, following directly from or, more correctly perhaps, resulting simultaneously with, the limitation of presence in regard to Duration, and leading to the necessity of being confined to a restricted area and therefore of being subject to cause and condition so as to be compelled to operate, or have experiences, under restricting conditions of cause, sequence, occasion and so on—such conditions never existing where there is no limitation of presence as regards either duration or extension. Technically it is called Niyati; lit. Restriction, or Regulation. (The determinant of 'where').

28. (*c*) Limitation in regard to Interest, leading to the necessity of *attending* to one or a few things at a time and thus of being *attached* to some, and letting go the others *i. e.* to the necessity of selection; technically Rāga; lit. Attachment or Interest.

29. (*d*) Limitation as regards simple Awareness, without reference to interest, feeling and so on, so as to be aware of only a few things *i. e.* to have only a limited sphere of cognition; technically Vidyā *i. e.* Knowledge (but limited knowledge).[1]

30. (*e*) Limitation as regards Authorship or power to accomplish, leading to the necessity of limited activity, so as *not* to be able to do, *i. e.* create,

1. Comp. ज्ञानं बन्धः (*Shiva Sūtra*, i. 2) where ज्ञान, knowledge, means limited knowledge only.

modify or destroy anything or everything at will; technically Kalā, lit. Art *i. e.* the power of limited creation.

The above are collectively called the five Kañchukas *i. e.* sheaths or cloaks of the Puruṣha.[1]

31. The generally limiting, self-forgetting and differentiating Power—technically Māyā.

This also is sometimes included in the Kañchukas which then are counted as six.

VIII. Five Principles of the *Universal* subject-object, *viz:*

32. The Principle of Correlation in the universal *experience*, *i. e.* in feeling and consciousness, between the experiencer and the experienced—technically the Sad-Vidyā or Shuddha-Vidyā *i. e.* True or pure Knowledge.

33. The Principle of Identification in the universal experience between what are thus correlated—technically the Aishvara or the Īshvara Tattva; lit. the 'Lordliness' or Might.

34. The Principle of Being—technically the Sādākhya, (or the Sadā Shiva Tattva); lit. that from which or in which the experience of Being begins.[2]

35. The Principle of Negation and Potentialisation, namely, of the Universal experience, *i. e.* the

---

1. The order in which the five Kañchukas are enumerated here is that of the *Īsh. Pra. Vṛitti* by Utpalachārya himself. In other works they are enumerated in the following order:—Kalā, Vidyā, Rāga, Kāla and Niyati.

2. Not unlike ब्रह्मन् of the Vedānta in its aspect only as Sat.

experience *of* and *as* the Universe;—technically the Shakti Tattva, *i. e.* the Power-Principle.[1]

36. The Principle of the pure Experiencer by itself, with all experience of objects and means of experiencing them entirely negatived and suppressed, *i. e.* the principle of pure 'I', without the experience of even an 'am' as formulated in the experience 'I am';—technically the Shiva Tattva; lit. the Benign Principle.[2]

What these Tattvas really are will, as said above, soon be made clear. For the present it is enough for our purpose to know that the manifested Universe consists, from the Trika point of view, of the above general factors or Tattvas; and that the Universe constituted of these factors is only a manifestation of the Power or Shakti of Parama Shiva, or, more correctly perhaps, of Parama Shiva himself in his aspect as Shakti.

THE PROCESS OF MANIFESTATION

Now, the manifestation of such a Universe, when regarded from the Trika point of view, is and can be but an expression of the ideas, or, more correctly, the experience, of Parama Shiva, the highest Reality, who is nothing but Chaitanya, pure and simple; and, as such, the process of Universal manifestation is, from this point of view, what may be called a process of experiencing out.

And if so, this process of Universal manifestation is, as is also obvious, the same as, or similar to, the psychical process in our daily lives of thinking and experiencing *out*, that is to say, of what may be called psychical Reproduction, (or *mental* Reproduction, using the word mental

1. Comp. the Vedāntic ब्रह्मन् as आनन्द only.

2. It may be said to correspond to Brahman as only Chit.

in the widest sense).[1] Technically the process is called one of 'Shining out'—Ābhāsana or Ābhāsa,[2]—and is in reality only a form of what in the Vedānta is called the 'Vivarta' *i. e.* the whirling or unrolling out, in other words, *appearing* in diverse forms. The only difference there is between the two may be stated as follows:—

The *appearances* are, according to the exponents of the 'Vivarta,' mere 'names and forms' (Nāma-Rūpa-mātra), and can under no circumstances be regarded as Real in the true sense of the word, namely, with an essence in them, *i. e.*, as part of them, which is *absolutely* unchanging and *never* non-existent. They are not essentially real because they are for ever non-existent in the Supreme Reality *i. e.* in Brahman, as the Reality in the Vedānta is termed—are never experienced in true Freedom, *i. e.* in Mokṣha, wherein absolute oneness with the Reality is realised. And being thus non-existent in the Real, they are not of the nature of Reality in their essential character. Nor are they absolutely unreal, because they form a beginningless series as facts of experience in

---

1. That is to say Unmeṣha, which is described as follows:

एकचिन्ताप्रसक्तस्य यतः स्यादपरोदयः ।
उन्मेषः स तु विज्ञेयः स्वयं तमुपलक्षयेत् ॥ *Spa. Kā.*, 41.

"That [process] is to be known as Unmeṣha (lit. the Opening out, like that of a bud into a full blossomed flower) whereby there arises [in the mind], engaged (or absorbed) in some one thought, some other thought [spontaneously by itself]. One should realise it oneself (*i. e.* by personal experience)."

Comp. also the *Spanda Sandoha* on it.

2. तत्र आभासरूपा एव जडचेतनपदार्थाः । *Pra. Vim.*, III. I. i. Comp. आभासन in *Pra. Hṛid.*, Su. 11. (p. 24.) with comm. on it. The doctrine of regarding Ābhāsa as the process of Manifestation is called Ābhāsa–Vāda, or Ābhāsa-Paramārtha-Vāda and also Svātantrya-Vāda; for instance in *Spanda Sandoha*. See also extract made in note 1. pp. 55, 56.

all stages and forms of existence short of Mokṣha, or that absolute Freedom and Independence which is constituted by the realisation, *in experience* (*i. e.* not merely as an intellectual conviction, a logical conclusion or a matter of faith), of one's absolute oneness with and *as* Brahman. The Nāma-Rūpas are—or rather Māyā, of which they are but forms, is—what cannot have applied to it the predications of absolutely real or absolutely unreal, of Being or not-Being (Sadasadbhyām anirvāchyā).

The teachers of the Ābhāsa process, on the other hand, maintain that the appearances *are* real in the sense that they are aspects of the ultimately Real, *i. e.*, of Parama Shiva. They are indeed non-existent in the Real *in and as the forms* in which we limited beings experience them. But they are not absolutely non-existent. They exist in the Real in a supremely synthesised form—as the *experience* which the Reality *as such, i. e. as* Parama Shiva, has. The appearances thus are *essentially* real as well. What in their essence and in the most highly synthesised form constitutes the experience of the Real cannot itself be unreal. For that would mean that the experience of the Real itself *as* the Real is unreal, which is absurd. The appearances therefore are not the forms of some indescribable, sadasadbhyām anirvāchyā, Māyā, but real, Sat, in essence.[1]

With only this difference between them, the two processes of Ābhāsa and Vivarta may be said to be practically the same. They are really one and the same process in so far as it is a *process* only—without reference to the ultimate nature of what that process brings about, *i.e.* of the 'appearances' constituting the Universe.

And as a process it may be described, if not defined, as that whereby products are brought into manifestation

1. इदं विश्वं......एकस्यां वा परस्यां पारमेश्वर्यां भैरवसंविदि अविभागेन बोधा-

from a source which, while giving birth to these, remains as unaffected and undivided as it ever was.[1] Further, it is a process of *apparent* division, so that, when divided, the source, instead of undergoing any diminution, *appears* to gain in strength, substance and even volume, if such an expression can be used with regard to what is really beyond measure.

An illustration in this latter aspect of the operation of the process, that is to say, the apparent strengthening of the source even when it seems to be divided may be found in that emotional expansion which has been so

---

त्मकेन रूपेण आस्ते—

वर्तमानावभासानां भावानामवभासनम् ।
अन्तःस्थितवतामेव घटते बहिरात्मना ॥ *Ī. Pra.*, 32.

उन्मीलनम् अवस्थितस्यैव प्रकटीकरणम् । *Pra. Hṛid.*, p. 6.

विवर्तो हि असत्यरूपनिर्भासात्मा इत्युक्तं; निर्भासते च असत्यं च इति कथमिति न चिन्तितम् । परिणामे तु रूपान्तरं तिरोभवति, रूपान्तरं प्रादुर्भवतीत्युक्तं; प्रकाशस्य तु रूपान्तराभावात् तत्तिरोधाने स्यादान्ध्यम्; अप्रकाशश्च प्रादुर्भवन् नैव प्रकाशेत इत्युभयथापि सुप्तं जगत् स्यात् इति न पर्यालोचितम् । प्रतिबिम्बवादे च स्वच्छतामात्रं संवेदनस्य न स्वातंत्र्यम् इति तत्समर्पकवस्त्वन्तरपर्येषणा कर्तव्या । अविद्या अनिर्वाच्या वैचित्र्यं च आधत्ते इति व्याहतम् । पारमेश्वरी शक्तिरेव इयमिति हृदयावर्जकः क्रमः । तस्मात् अनपह्नवनीयः प्रकाशविमर्शात्मा संवित्स्वभावः परमशिवो भगवान् स्वातन्त्र्यादेव रुद्रादिस्थावरान्तप्रमातृरूपतया नीलसुखादिप्रमेयतया च अनतिरिक्तयापि अतिरिक्तयेव स्वरूपानाच्छादिकया संवित्स्वरूपनान्तरीयकस्वातन्त्र्यमहिम्ना प्रकाशते इत्ययं स्वातन्त्र्यवादः प्रोन्मीलितः । *Pra. vi. vi.*

आभासपरमार्थवादः आभासवादो वा । *Sp. Sand.*, Fol. 3.
तत्र आभासरूपा एव जडचेतनपदार्थाः । *Pra. vi.*, III. ii. 1.
यद् यद् आभाति तत् तत् सृज्यते । *Pra. Hṛid.*, p. 25.

1. Comp. *Shiva Dṛiṣhṭi* where this characteristic is clearly shown, when it is stated how, on the manifestation of the successive Tattvas, the preceding ones are in no way affected. Comp. also the following striking couplet embodying the Vedāntic view of the question :

पूर्णमदः पूर्णमिदं पूर्णात्पूर्णमुदच्यते ।
पूर्णस्य पूर्णमादाय पूर्णमेवावशिष्यते ॥ (Shāntipāṭha.)

beautifully expressed by the immortal Kalidāsa in the following lines:—

रथाङ्गनाम्नोरिव भावबन्धनं
बभूव यत् प्रेम परस्पराश्रयम् ।
विभक्तमप्येकसुतेन तत् तयोः
परस्परस्योपरि पर्यचीयत ॥

" That love of theirs (of King Dilīpa and his queen Sudakshiṇā) which, like the ideally loving union of a couple of chakora birds, had (hitherto) been resting only in themselves (the love of the one entwining round the other only, without a rivalry), although (now) shared with a son, —that love of theirs, inspite of this division as to its object, only increased for each other." [1]

Such a statement may sound a paradox and a contradiction in itself; but we all know that real love and other emotions not only show no signs of diminution when distributed and divided over an increasing number of objects but they only grow in volume and expansion, while the source from which they spring remains inexhaustible.

A Hindu philosophic thinker can also recognise, in the process of the growth and expansion of a vital cell, an instance of the operation of the Vivarta or the Ābhāsa. Here is a cell which is a sensible object with a something called life in it. As it grows and expands, it divides and multiplies itself. But how? Has there been a real division in the *life* also which was manifest in the first cell? If so, how is there no diminution in the life which is perceived in each of the new cells? How is it that there is *as much* of life in *each* of the new cells as there was in the original one, if there has been a real division in the *life* itself? From the Hindu point of view the division is only apparent; and, although numerous other centres of life may be produced from a single

---

1. *Raghuvaṁsha*, iii. 24.

centre, the life itself is not really divided but remains ever the same in every one of the newly produced centres.

These two cases may be regarded as examples of the Ābhāsa process in its aspect as production, or reproduction and expansion, *without any real division.*

But, as said above, Ābhāsa has another aspect also. In this aspect it is a process whereby, while the products come into manifestation, their source remains entirely unaffected and exists exactly as it ever was as the inexhaustible fountain-head of an infinite series of such products. The process of vital cell-division would be an illustration of this aspect also of the Ābhāsa, if we could observe the real source of not only the life we perceive in a cell but of all life. As however, this is not possible for all of us at this stage of human growth and evolution —it is the true masters of Yoga who alone can be said to possess this power of observation—we may have to seek elsewhere for a really satisfactory example of the Ābhāsa in all its aspects. But without being able to observe the source of all life, we may safely assert that even the immediate source of the life in the progeny—the vitality of the parent—is little affected when the offspring is given birth to, and that the reproduction of life by a parent is an instance, however imperfect, of the Ābhāsa process.

We should find a good example of Ābhāsa in some of the recent findings of abnormal psychology, as it is now being studied in the West, *if* these findings were universally recognised as facts. The instance of what has been called the 'dissociation of a personality,' taken along with what has been named the subliminal self of a man, would furnish an excellent example of what is meant by Ābhāsa. For, in such a case, we could see how a number of 'personalities'—distinct individuals to all intents and purposes—is produced from apparently the one and only subliminal self which itself is not evidently affected in any way even when a number of offshoots, so clearly differentiated and separated off from one another, is produced from it.[1]

But what would seem to furnish a remarkably satisfactory example of the Ābhāsa, indeed would prove to certain minds its existence and operation in nature, may probably be found in the latest theory of Western Science as to the ultimate constitution of matter, when that theory is fully established and accepted on all hands. From what one understands of this theory, one would not be far wrong in saying that it is tending in a direction which would seem to point to the conclusion that perceptible matter will at last have to be regarded as somehow a product of a something which fills and pervades all space that we know,—that matter in its ultimate form is nothing more than may be mere 'places or centres of strain' in the all-filling Something.

But how, even as 'centres of strain' only, can Matter be produced from this Something? The 'Something' must be regarded as a Continuum and even a Plenum.[2] It cannot be divided up and parcelled out, and a bit of it located here and another bit placed there, as matter can be. Nor can it, as a plenum and a continuum, *really* be *changed*—even if it be 'strained'—into some thing else, specially a something which is divisible and capable of allocation in disjointed sections of space, as Matter, its product, is. The production of Matter from the Something then must be by a process which, while bringing the product into existence, leaves the source of the product unchanged,—in short it is the Vivarta or the Ābhāsa process. Here then we have a remarkable

1. See *Multiple Personality* by Drs. Sidis and Goodhart.

2. For reasons see *Hindu Realism* pp. 47-49.

illustration of what the Hindu Philosophers mean when they speak of the Vivarta or Ābhāsa.

However this may be, what we have to note here is (*a*) that the process of the universal manifestation,—technically called Ābhāsa,—as regarded by the Trika, is one which, while bringing the product into existence does not in any way affect the source from which it is produced, the source remaining as unchanged as it ever was; and (*b*) that it is a process of only apparent division.

And this is so because the universal manifestation consists merely in an experiencing out, inasmuch as the ultimate source of the Universe is a Reality which is a purely Experiencing Principle, and as, there being no other ingredient whatsoever which does or can ever enter into the composition of the Universe, the process of production or reproduction on the part of an Experiencing Principle by itself is incapable of having any other meaning than the multiplication of thoughts, ideas, feelings and the like, *i. e.*, having various experiences. The process therefore is essentially one which, as said before, may be likened to what may be called a psychical, rather a logical, process in our daily lives; and as such its operation is marked by steps or stages, which follow one another as logical necessities—each successive step following inevitably from the one preceding it, as the deduction of a certain conclusion of a particularised kind follows inevitably, in a rationally thinking mind, from certain premises of a general type. That is to say the operation of the process is guided by a law of logical necessity.[1]

And the way in which this law of a logical necessity operates, and the actual results to which it leads as the manifestation of the Universe proceeds, and how finally

1. See *ante* verse quoted in note 1, p. 54. Comp. also the Hegelian doctrine of the Universe being the immanent logical dialectic of the Absolute.

each successive result, when thus produced, in no way affects the preceding one or ones from which it follows, may be shown as follows ;—[1]

THE TRANSCENDENT PARAMA SHIVA

First,—*i. e.*, logically but not in *time*—[2] there is Parama Shiva who is of the nature of Bliss itself and all complete in himself. He holds in himself the still unmanifested Universe as an idea, rather, as an experience of his own which is also the root of all that afterwards becomes expressible in terms of discursive thought and speech[3]. At the same time He transcends even this supremely ideal Universe or, which is the same thing, this Universal experience.

So long as He is this, that is, so long as He is both the transcending Reality, Bliss and Intelligence as well as the one all-including Supreme Experience of the perfect, because the supremely ideal, Universe, there is no need of a Universal manifestation. For there is, as it were, no feeling of a *want*, Parama Shiva being all-complete in Himself.

---

1. For some of the texts on which the whole of this section is based see Appendix III.

2. There is as yet no experience of 'Time' as we understand it. 'Time,' as a succession of moments, is experienced only with the manifestation of the 26th Tattva *i. e.* with Kāla; see *ante* p. 51 and below p. 78. This is a point which should be borne very carefully in mind if one is to avoid confusion. Of course in speaking even of a purely logical process one has to use such phrases as 'before', 'after', 'now' and so on. But it should be understood that this is so only because we cannot speak otherwise, and that the experience of Time which such phrases imply does not begin till we come to the 26th Tattva in this list.

3. Parama Shiva holds the universe as an आमर्शः परनादगर्भः ।

Five Principles of the Universal Subject-Object

The Shiva Tattva

But, in order that there may be a Universe, He brings into operation that aspect of his Shakti which manifests itself as the principle of *Negation*[1] and lets the ideal Universe disappear from His view and allows Himself, as it were, to feel the *want* of a Universe, but for which feeling there could be, as said above, no need of a manifested Universe on the part of one who is all-complete in Himself.

In this state He is what He was as Parama Shiva in all essentials and in every respect, with only the elimination of the experience of the ideal Universe which Parama Shiva, in His aspect as pervading the Universe,—as distinguished from the transcending aspect,—feels as one and identical with himself.

The experience of this state is called the Shiva Tattva which comes into manifestation without in any way whatsoever affecting Parama Shiva who remains as He ever was—exactly and in every respect the same as before—existing simultaneously with and including the Shiva Tattva.

With the experience of the supremely ideal Universe negatived, the Shiva Tattva is only the pure light of Intelligence (Chinmātra, Chit only) without anything

---

1. निषेधव्यापाररूपा । Comm. on *Par. Sār.*, Kā. 4.

श्रीपरमशिवः स्वात्मैक्येन स्थितं विश्वम्........अवबिभावयिषुः पूर्वं चिदैक्याख्यातिमयानाश्रित-शिव-पर्याय-**शून्यातिशून्यात्मतया** प्रकाशाभेदेन प्रकाशमानतया स्फुरति; ततः चिद्–रसाश्यानतारूपाशेषतत्त्व-भुवन-भाव-तत्तत्प्रमात्राद्यात्मतयापि प्रथते ॥ *Pra. Hṛid.*, pp. 8, 9.

तान् असद्रूपान्; *Shaivī Ṭīkā.*

Comp. Schelling and Fichte, among others, on this point.

whatsoever to shine upon—without even a trace of the notion or feeling of a Universe in the experience[1]. It is thus only the pure '*I*' without even the thought or feeling 'I *am*,' for 'am' or being implies a relation, namely, *of identity*, howsoever subdued or indistinct, meaning I am *this*, viz., this body or this mind and so on; or I am *here* and *now*, which however really means I am *what* is here and now, *i. e.*, I am *this* something which is here and now. But as there is in this state no notion or feeling of a 'this' or 'that' (of an 'idam', meaning, as it would in this state, the ideal Universe), there can be no thought of even an 'am' or *being* in the experience of the Shiva Tattva. It is therefore the experience which acts as the Principle of the pure 'I'[2].

Thus Shiva Tattva is the first stage[3] in the process of the Universal manifestation; and it is a state in which the Chit aspect of Shakti is most manifest, all the other aspects being no doubt *there*, but held as it were in suppression or suspense[4].

The Shakti Tattva

And because these other aspects of the Divine Shakti are held in suppression—and because, indeed, the whole experience of the supremely ideal Universe of the Parama Shiva state is negatived and held as suppressed—there must be *some* aspect of this Divine Shakti herself in operation to make such a tremendous act of Negation possible. This the Universe-negativing aspect of the

---

1. प्रकाशाभेदेन प्रकाशमानतया स्फुरति। *Ante* p. 62, note. 1.

2. अनन्योन्मुखः अहंप्रत्ययः; *Pra. Vim.*; III. i. 3.

3. See, however, below p. 65, note 1.

4. This is following Abhinava Gupta. According to Utpala, however, इच्छाशक्तिमयः शिवः; Comm. on *Shiva Dṛiṣhṭi*, ii. 1. But then Utpala counts only three aspects of the Shakti as primary in which the other two, Chit and Ānanda are merged.

Divine Shakti is called the *Shakti Tattva*, which is to be distinguished from Shakti as such, and is thus the second element or factor which enters into the composition of the manifested Universe. It can scarcely be called a second stage as it comes into manifestation simultaneously with the Shiva Tattva. Indeed, it may be safely said that it is by the operation of the Shakti Tattva that the manifestation of the Shiva Tattva becomes at all possible. And it is on account of this fact perhaps, that the separate mention of the Shakti Tattva is sometimes omitted from the list of Tattvas, it being counted as one with and included in the Shiva Tattva [1].

But if counted separately, it is really the manifestation of the Ānanda aspect of the Divine Shakti; for the nature of Ānanda, as perfect Bliss and Supremest Self-satisfaction, is absolute Rest in what is one's own, and cessation of all flutter and movement.[2] For no perfect Bliss is ever there unless there is complete absence of restlessness—unless there is a cessation of all goings and movings out. As there is, in the stage we are considering, absolutely no such moving out yet, but only the feeling of absolute rest and peace in one's own real self, this feeling can be only the realisation of the Ānanda aspect of the Divine Shakti [3].

Thus as they come into manifestation, the Shiva and the Shakti Tattvas remain united to each other—the one as the pure light of the Experiencing Principle, as only the Chit, realising itself as only the pure 'I', without the experience of even an 'am', much less of a Universe which that light can shine upon and reveal; and the

1. See, among others, *Pra. Hṛid.*, p. 8.

2. आनन्द or Love is really स्वरूपविश्रान्ति; *ante* p. 44, note 2.

3. हृदयं परमेशितुः; हृदयम् 'heart' really means love, joy and bliss. The Shakti Tattva is really the Universe as a *potentiality*. It is the योनि or बीजावस्था as referred to in *Pra. Hṛid.*, Sū. 11., p. 24.

other as the realisation of the feeling of only the profoundest Bliss and Peace passing all understanding—as that Ānanda which is to be the core of all things to come.

Although produced, *in a sense*, from Parama Shiva, inasmuch as they form an experience which is other than and distinct from the Supremest Experience, the Parā Saṁvit, of and as Parama Shiva the Shiva-Shakti Tattvas are really eternally existent [1]. For they do not disappear in Pralaya but remain in the bosom of Parama Shiva as the seed of the Universe to come. If this analogy of the seed may be carried a little further, then the Shiva Tattva is what may be called the Life (Prāṇa) in the Universal seed, while the Shakti Tattva abides as the potentiality of the infinite variety of Forms in which that Life becomes manifest in a Universe.

Further, the Shiva Tattva, as life (or Prāṇa) in this sense, is the very 'first flutter,' of Parama Shiva,—the first 'vibratory movement' towards a Universal manifestation; and the Shakti Tattva is what checks, controls and regulates that movement of Life and acts as the Principle of Restraint. [2]

The Sādākya Tattva

From the Shiva-Shakti State there gradually develops the experience which may be formulated in thought as '*I am.*'

---

1. See, for instance, *Pra. Hṛid.*, p. 8, where the Shiva-Tattva (in which the Shakti-Tattva also is included there) is shown as quite outside the range of the Tattvas which come into manifestation only at Sṛiṣhṭi. See also *Shiva Dṛiṣhṭi*, *Īsh. Pra. Kā.* (III. i. 1) &c. where the manifestation of the Sadā Shiva Tattva is counted as the first.

2. यदयमनुत्तरमूर्तिर्निजेच्छया निखिलमिदं जगत् स्रष्टुम् ।
पस्पन्दे स स्पन्दः प्रथमः शिवतत्त्वमुच्यते तज्ज्ञैः ॥ *Tattva-Sand.* 1.
प्रथमः स्पन्द is here nothing more than the first flutter of life.

This experience of an 'I am' means and must mean, as said above, 'I am *this*'—the 'this' in the state we are considering being of course an indistinct, because not as yet clearly formulated, reference in thought and feeling to the Ideal Universe which was suppressed in the Shiva-Shakti stage, but is just beginning to come up to the surface of the experience again, like an object which, being of a naturally buoyant character but having remained submerged under pressure, may begin to float up to the surface of the ocean as the pressure is lifted. The Ideal Universe at this stage is felt, as it were, as a vague something just stirring in the depth of one's consciousness[1]—as a movement, as it were, of an unformulated thought, or an undefined feeling, of a something in one's innermost being as yet eluding a clear grasp in experience. And as it begins to stir there, the experiencer also begins as it were to recollect his true character and state, in somewhat the same way as a man may begin to recollect, as he just begins to recover from a state, let us say of supreme joy (as, for instance, when one may be 'in the embrace of the beloved')[2] which has made him forget everything *about* himself—his own status, position, possessions and glory—and may just *vaguely begin* to formulate these in thought as "I *am so and so*," the 'so

---

1. निमेषोऽन्तः सदाशिवः; *Ish. Prat.*, III. i. 3.

2. Shakti is the Hṛidaya, the 'heart', *i. e.* the 'Beloved', of the Supreme Experiencer, हृदयं परमेशितुः; *Parā. Prāv.* Comp. also

स ह एतावान् आस यथा स्त्रीपुमांसौ सम्परिष्वक्तौ ।

"He (the Ātman) was as much as a man and wife in each other's embrace are". *Bṛih. Up.*, I. iv. 3.

तद्यथा प्रियया स्त्रिया सम्परिष्वक्तो न बाह्यं किञ्चन वेद नान्तरम्, एवमेव अयं पुरुषः प्राज्ञेनात्मना सम्परिष्वक्तो न बाह्यं किञ्चन वेद नान्तरम् ।

"Now as a man, when embraced by his beloved wife, knows nothing that is without, nothing that is within, thus does the Purusha, when embraced by the Prājña Ātman, know nothing that is without, nothing that is within." *Ibid.*, IV. iii. 21.

and so' being as yet of an undefined character but referring all the same to his bodily form, name and their relations to things, in other words, to what constitutes the 'this' in the thought or feeling of the 'I am' on his part.

This stage follows the former one as a necessity by virtue of what may be called a law similar to the one, which, in the psychical process of the human mind, brings about a stage of 'movement' *after* a state of profound but calm and motionless enjoyment of perfect *bliss*, *rest* and *peace*. It is due, one might say, to the stirring anew of the Life of the Universe which was held in suppression in the previous stage.

It is, however, just the beginning of activity—of just the first stirring of life—and therefore the thought or feeling of the Ideal Universe at this stage is, as said above, only a dim one, like a faint and indistinct picture of a long-forgotten scene which is beginning to re-form itself in one's memory and is still quite in the background of consciousness. This being the situation at this stage, the realisation of the 'I',—in the experience 'I am this,'—is a *more dominant* factor, than the 'this' referring to the Ideal Universe which is just beginning to reappear in consciousness and is, as a consequence, still very vague and indistinct.

It is also the state in which there is for the first time the notion of 'being' in the experience 'I *am* this,' and is therefore called the Sādākhya[1]—that in which there is for the first time the experience which may be spoken of as Being. It is also called the Sadā Shiva *Tattva*, which as only another name of the Sādākhya should be distinguished from Sadā Shiva the meaning of which term by itself will be explained later.

It is the state in which the Ichchhā aspect of the Divine Shakti is the dominant feature, the others being

1. सदाख्यायां भवं, यतः प्रभृति सदिति प्रख्या. । *Prat. Vim.*, III. i. 2.

held in suppression[1]. And it is only natural that this should be so. For, as already said, Ichchhā is the aspect which, in one of its forms, produces, or rather *is*, that feeling which may be described as one of divine ' wonder ' as to what to do—of *resolve* as to what is to be done; and as such *precedes* actual movement and activity. And as there is as yet no actual activity but only a sense of wonder of this sort as to what to do and a resolve to move and act—only a *will* to act, following a state of perfect Rest and Bliss—it is naturally a state in which the Ichchhā aspect of the Divine Shakti is most manifest.[2]

As the manifestation of the Ichchhā aspect of the Divine Shakti, the Sādākhya, or the Sadā Shiva Tattva, may perhaps be also spoken of as the state of Self-realisation as ' Being ' or ' Force ' which is *able* to start action. This Self-realisation as Being and Force—or, as it may be said of it at a lower stage, of realising one-self as a *somebody* with a *will* that is *able* to perform an act—is a necessary step before that act itself can be undertaken.

That this is the case may be seen from an analysis of our daily experiences under circumstances which are at least to some extent similar to those we are now considering. It is true that in our daily life the process of such a realisation as being or as a *somebody* able to do a thing—or, as may be said of it, such a mental stock-taking of one-self *as a being with a will*,—is a very rapid one, almost too rapid to be clearly realised. But it is all the same there. And the Sādākhya step in the life process of the Universe may be said to correspond to this step in the daily life of a man. It is a necessary step, without which no act of the kind that is going to follow is possible.

1. According to Utpala, however, सदाशिव is ज्ञानशक्तिमान् while इच्छाशक्ति is man ifest in the Shiva Tattva. Utpala on *Shiva Dṛiṣhṭi*, ii. 1.

2. It is a 'static' condition preceding the 'kinetic state' of actual movement.

Further, although counted as the third Tattva, the Sādākhya is, as a matter of fact, the first manifestation in the Universal process. For, as pointed out above, the Shiva-Shakti Tattvas are really eternally existent.

And the Sādākhya comes into manifestation, as will be readily seen, from what has been said of it, as the principle of pure Being.

The Aishvara Tattva

In the next stage, this 'mental stock-taking,' on the part of the Divine Experiencer as a Being with a will to act, is followed by the emerging out, as the most prominent element in the Experience, of the 'this,' that is, of the Ideal Universe which had been lurking as an indistinct picture in the back-ground of the Being. In this stage, therefore, the experience assumes a form which may be formulated in thought as: '*This* am I',—a form in which the 'this' becomes the more dominant element, while the other factor, the 'I,' is thrown into the back-ground. Self-realisation as being is followed by the realisation—by a full *survey*—of what constitutes the *state* of that Self as Being.

We may observe in our own individual lives a state corresponding to this one in the process of the Universal manifestation. It may be noticed that, as one begins to think of oneself, after an enjoyment of the all-forgetting bliss of the 'beloved's embrace' of our previous illustration, the vague experience of the 'so and so' in the thought 'I am so and so,' which first emerges into consciousness, is followed by a clear notion of who or what he really is. He begins to realise clearly all about himself—his state, in short.

And it is obvious that in this experience what is more dominant is not the notion of the 'I' as a being or a mere somebody, which is there only as a back-ground, but the notion of what constitutes the 'so and so' or the 'this,' *i. e.*, his state. His experience in this state is occupied chiefly with a *survey* of what may be called his 'so-and-so-ness' which emerges into full view and eclipses and *Identified* with what may be termed his *I-ness.*

Thus, the state which follows the Sadā-Shiva Tattva in the life-process of the Universe is brought about in obedience to what may be called a law similar to the one which obtains in our own individual lives under similar or somewhat similar circumstances.

This stage of making a full *survey* of, *Identification* with, what constitutes the state of the Experiencer, —of the 'this' aspect of his being,—namely, of the Ideal Universe as it must be at this stage, is called the Aishvara or the Īshvara Tattva, *i. e.*, the Tattva of realising what constitutes the Lordliness and the Glory of the Divine Being. The 'Īshvara *Tattva*' is to be distinguished from Īshvara, the Lord, to be explained later —like the Sadā-Shiva *Tattva* from Sadā-Shiva mentioned above.

And as it is the state in which a full survey of the 'This' *i. e.*, the Ideal Universe is taken,—in which the 'This' emerges into full and clear view, as a clear and well defined picture and not as a vague and indistinct image in the back-ground of one's consciousness as it is in the Sādākhya state,—the aspect of the Divine Shakti which is most manifest in this state, is the Jñāna or Power of being conscious[1].

In these two states, the Sādākhya and the Aishvara,— or the Sadā-Shiva Tattva and the Īshvara Tattva—the

1. But according to Utpala उद्रिक्तक्रियाशक्तिरीश्वरः । It is सदाशिव that in Utpala's view is ज्ञानशक्तिमान्; *Shiva Dṛiṣhṭi Vṛitti*, ii. 1. ज्ञान is आमर्षकता; आमर्ष is again defined, as said above (p. 45 note 1), as ईषत्तया वेद्योन्मुखता ।

experience may, as said above, be respectively formulated in thought as

'I am This'
and 'This am I,'

with only this difference that, while in the first case the 'I'-side or aspect of the relation of *being* is more dominant, the 'This'-side remaining merely as a vague background, in the second state, that of the Aishvara, the 'This'-side of the relation is the more prominent aspect, the 'I'-side being thrown quite into the back-ground, indeed, being quite *Identified* with and merged into the 'This.'[1]

The Sad-Vidya

In the next state which follows, there arises an equalisation in prominence of the two aspects of the Experience which then takes the form, 'I am This' in which both the 'I' and the 'This' are realised with equal clearness, so much so that, while they are felt as entirely identified with each other, they can yet be clearly separated in thought—so that the 'I' can be realised as the subject and the 'This' as the object of the experience, and that, for this reason, the experiencing subject can realise the 'This' as 'my' and 'mine,' in much the same way as a man in his daily life, while ordinarily feeling himself as one and identified with his body, thoughts and feelings, yet somehow realises himself as the possessor of these and speaks of them as this is '*my*' body or these thoughts and feelings are 'mine[2].'

This experience of equalising the realisation of the two sides of the relation of identity, namely, 'I am This', and also of what may be called possession—of one of the two sides as *belonging* to the other—is called the Sad

---

1. Comp. ईश्वरो बहिरुन्मेषः; *Īsh. Prat.*, III. i. 3.
2. सामानाधिकरण्यं हि सद्विद्याहमिदंद्वयोः; *Īsh. Prat.*, III. i. 3.

Vidyā or Shuddha Vidyā—the state of Experience (or knowledge) in which the *true* relation of things is realised.

That such a state follows and must follow the previous ones may be seen from our own individual experiences in similar circumstances.

From the balancing in realisation of the two factors, the 'I' and the 'This,' of the experience in this state, and from simultaneously realising the one as belonging to the other, there also follows an important result; namely, there arises, for the first time, what may be called the Experience of diversity-in-unity-and-identity (Bhedābheda)[1]. This new Experience may really be said to correspond at a lower stage, as just stated, to the one which enables an individual human being to regard his body and thoughts and feelings as at once diverse and different from and yet one and identical with himself, and to think and speak of their totality as at once 'I' and 'mine.' This Experience arises in the Shuddha Vidyā State because, as the Experiencer has his attention—or what corresponds to it in a lower state—drawn equally to himself as the 'I' of the Experience and to the 'This' as what we have called the object of the Experience, he naturally realises, on the one hand, *some* contrast between the 'I', which is felt as an absolutely undivided *Unity*, and the 'This', which, as the prototype of the *multifariousness* in the future Universe of the sensible and psychical experience, is seen as other than such a Unity—as a something which has in it at least the germs of diversity;—and, on the other, feels that this is yet somehow one and identical with himself, as being really nothing else than his own Experience, *i. e.* his own thoughts and feelings, if we may use such terms in this connection. In our individual lives also as ordinary human beings, the

1. Or, as it is also called, 'परापरदशा'; *Īsh. Prat.*, III. i. 5. Comp. also भेदाभेदविमर्शनात्मकमन्त्ररूपा (सद्विद्या); *Svachchh.*, iv. 95.

corresponding experience of diversity-in-unity-and-identity in regard to the body and thoughts and feelings is possible, because, while our attention is simultaneously drawn, willingly or unwillingly, to what, on the one hand, is realised as the 'I' and, on the other, to the thoughts, feelings and bodily states, a contrast is, as a consequence of this simultaneous noticing of the dual factors of the Experience, also felt—the 'I' being felt as a Unity and the rest as a diversity and yet as somehow one and identical with the unity of the 'I.'

Such an Experience is possible in the Shuddha Vidyā State, and not in the previous ones, because in these latter the 'attention' of the Experiencer is, as it were, one sided. In the Sadā Shiva Tattva it is drawn chiefly to the 'I'-side, while in the Īshvara Tattva the 'gaze' is fixed principally on the 'This'-side—on what constitutes the Aishvarya, *i. e.*, the Lordly State, of the Experiencer. There is, therefore, in these states, little chance of what may be called a comparison between the two aspects of the Experience 'I am This,' and therefore of realising both the contrast and the identity which there subsist between the two.

As another result of this realisation of contrast and of the experience of diversity-in-unity-and-identity, the 'This' of the experience is now realised as not a pure and undivided 'this' or a unit, but as a *whole, i. e.*, an 'All-this.'

Further, as the 'All-this' at this stage is of the nature of pure ideas,—of thoughts and feelings,—they are naturally realised as proceeding from, and originated and created by, the Experiencer himself, in much the same way as a limited human being realises his own thoughts and feelings as his own creations.

The whole Experience in this state, therefore, assumes a form which may be stated as follows:—

> *I am all-this and all-this is mine as part and parcel of myself* and all this proceeds from and is created by me—I am the author of all this[1].

In such an experience there is and must be, as is obvious, some movement of 'thought'—some *action.* There is, in the first place, a movement of 'attention' from the 'This' to the 'I', and again, as it were, all over and all round the 'This,' so as to realise it as an 'All-this' as distinguished from the bare 'This' of the previous state. This is all very different from the absolute hush and stillness of the divine wonder of the Sadā Shiva stage and also from that steady and immovable 'gaze' at the glory of the Divine State which there is in the Īshvara Tattva. While in these Tattvas there is thus motionlessness, there are in the Shuddha Vidyā state movement and action—or what, in a lower stage of manifestation, correspond to these. In the Shuddha Vidyā, therefore, the Kriyā aspect of the Divine Shakti is most manifest.[2]

So far, the manifestation of the Universe is a purely Ideal one; and being Ideal it is the 'Perfect and Pure Way or Order' (Shuddhādhvan) without any blemish in it. In these purely Ideal States of manifestation, *i. e.*, in the

---

1. It may perhaps be spoken of as the Universal Ahaṅkāra. Comp. सर्वो ममायं विभवः *Īsh. Prat.* IV. i. 12 as an expression of the experience of this state; also यथा द्वैतवादिनामीश्वरः in which terms the experiencer at this stage is described; *Pra. Vi.*, III. i. 6.

There is a slight difference in the definition given of Sad Vidyā in the various works on the Trika, and Utpala quotes several views of it. The definition and description given here are substantially those of Utpala and Abhinava Gupta.

2. But, as already pointed out, according to Utpala, Kriyā Shakti is manifest in the Īshvara Tattva. He, however, speaks of only three aspects of Shakti, *viz.* Ichchhā, Jñāna and Kriyā, the Chit and Ānanda aspects being regarded as

Pure Order, the things are realised as they *truly* are, and therefore they are the regions of pure and true knowledge (Sad Vidyā or Shuddha Vidyā.)

Moreover they are the manifestation of the Universal, as distinguished from the limited aspects of the Experience. That is to say, in these states the Experiencing entities are Universal beings who realise themselves actually *as such*, and have for their Experience the whole of the universal ' All-this,'—in different forms, no doubt, in the different states constituting the Pure Order, but, in no particular state, with any part of the ' This ' hidden away from them.

THE LIMITED INDIVIDUAL EXPERIENCE

Maya and Her Progeny: The Six Kanchukas

The manifestation which now, that is *after* the appearance of the Shuddha Vidyā, begins, is that of the Universe which constitutes the experience of *limited* beings, who, as such, realise not the whole of the universal ' All-this ' but only limited aspects of it, and who also regard themselves as mutually exclusive, limited entities. This latter manifestation may therefore be spoken of as the Limited process, as distinguished from the Universal process described above. And, as consisting of limited states of Experience, the manifestation from this point onward is called the Ashuddhādhvan—the Impure and Imperfect Way or Order—and also the Māyādhvan, the Māyā's Way, because the principle or factor which

---

included in these three. And the difference in his view of the severally manifested aspects of the Shakti in the several Tattvas may be due to this fact. The view given here of the several manifestations of the Shakti is that of Abhinava Gupta.

comes into manifestation as the first product of this Order, and which afterwards dominates all the rest of it, is what is called Māyā.

How what is essentially pure and perfect comes to be impure, and how 'evil'—as it is put—at all enters the Universe will be explained later. For the present it is enough for our purpose just to recognise that, from this stage onward, the manifestation is of a limited and, there fore, an imperfect and impure Order; and that the first product of this order is what is termed Māyā.

This Māyā is, as will be seen presently, what may be called a Force, namely, of obscuration[1]; and therefore, as a Force or Shakti, is and can be but an aspect of the Divine Shakti. Its chief function is to obscure and thereby limit the Experience in regard to the true nature of both what is experienced and the Experiencer himself.

And it comes into manifestation just at this stage for the same reasons and in obedience to the same or a similar law, as we find in operation in our daily lives under conditions which are also similar; namely, as we fall asleep[2], when, after the enjoyment of a thing for a while, our interest flags, or, after some activity, we are overtaken by a feeling of tiredness and lassitude, and the scene which we have been enjoying, or what we have been acting on, is obscured from our view.

Similarly, the All-Experiencer of the Shuddha Vidyā begins, when he has enjoyed the 'All-this' for a time, to feel as it were a sense of tiredness and lassitude—if it may be permitted to use such expressions in regard to the conditions of such an Ideal state of Experience. He

---

1. तिरोधांनंकरी मायाभिधा पुनः; *Īsh. Prat.*, III. i. 7.

For references to texts on the whole of this section on Māyā and the five other Kañchukas (*Viz.*, Kāla, Niyati, Rāga, Vidyā and Kalā) see Appendix IV.

2. Comp. सुप्तस्थानीयमणुम्; *Tantrasāra*, Āhn. 8.

is overtaken, in other words, by what must be a Power or Force. And it is this Force which is called Māyā. And, as he thus comes under the influence of Māyā, he as it were falls asleep, and the universal 'All-this' passes out of his view as a clear perception; that is to say, it is *obscured*, there arising in its place but an Experience, rather a *feeling*, of a *vague, indistinct and undefined something* which is practically the same as the *feeling* of a '*Nothing.*'

And as this happens, *i. e.*, as the All-Experiencer assumes an aspect of as it were falling asleep, the relations which it *previously* had with the 'All-this' are all changed.

Although countless in aspects, these relations of the Universal Experiencer of the Shuddha Vidya to the Universal 'All-this'—*prior* to the latter fading into an indistinct something—are, as clearly defined and distinct *types*, only five, and may be symbolised, in terms which are really only applicable in a lower stage of manifestation, as follows.

1. Co-evality or an alwaysness of presence with, and therefore of the experience of, the whole of the 'All-this;'—in Sanskrit, Nityatva. (lit. alwaysness or eternity).

2. Unrestricted access to and operation on the whole of the 'All-this', that is, *all-pervasiveness* or all-inclusiveness, without the necessity of being confined to a restricted area, and of having experiences therein under restricting conditions of cause, sequence, occasion and the like;—in Sanskrit, Vyāpakatva (lit. all-reachingness or all-obtainingness.)[1]

---

1. *I. e.* Omnipresence which, from one point of view, is presence in *all* space, and, from another, presence in *no space* *i. e.* transcending all space.

3. All-interestedness, that is, the relation of having an *equal* interest in, and therefore equally possessing and *enjoying*, the whole of the 'All-this'; that is to say *all-completeness* and therefore all-satisfaction, there remaining nothing outside its possession and therefore there being no feeling of want;—in Sanskrit, Pūrṇatva (lit. fullness).

4. All-consciousness, all-knowledge or all-vision, being conscious of the whole of the 'All-this';—in Sanskrit, Sarvajñatva, (lit. all-knowingness or omniscience.)

and 5. All-authorship;—in Sanskrit, Sarva-kartṛitva, (lit. all-makingness.)

Now, as the All-Experiencer assumes a 'sleepy' aspect, as he does under the influence of Māyā, and as, on this account, the 'All-this' begins to fade away from his vision, there takes place a *change* in his Experience; and, with the change thus brought about, there arises a change also in these five typical aspects of his relation to the 'All-this'. And they then become respectively the relations of

a. Time *i. e.* limited duration—that is to say the relation with the experienced as past, present and future (technically called Kāla; lit. counting or flowing. The determinant of When);

b. Restriction or Regulation, *viz.*, in regard to presence in space, *i. e.*, in regard to access, field of operation and so on, leading to the necessity of having experiences under the regulating conditions of cause, sequence, occasion and the like—such conditions never existing in the case of an Experiencing Being which is always and everywhere present with, or related to, everything, (technically, Niyati; lit. Restriction or Regulation. The determinant of Where);

c. Limited Interest, (technically, Rāga; lit. sticking to, attachment to something or somethings in particular, and therefore dissatisfaction, according as interest in one thing flags, as it does and must, and it moves on to another thing);

d. Limited Consciousness (*i. e.* pure awareness) or knowledge, (technically, Vidyā; lit. knowledge);[1]

and *e.* Limited Authorship, (technically, Kalā; lit. art or power of limited creation).

And this happens in the following way :—

In order to bring about the desired end, Māyā makes the Experiencer feel himself one with the experienced—the experienced which is no longer what it was in the Sādākhya and the Aishvara states, but is already perceived more or less as an Anātman or not-Self *i. e.* other than the Self of the Experience. This is necessary, because there can really be no change in the Experiencer himself—he being, by his very nature as Chaitanya, absolutely unchangeable. All change and limitation, therefore, which he may ever experience in regard to himself, as distinguished from the experienced, can be only of a super-imposed character—being really changes in the experienced when the latter is already perceived as a something other, or at least partially other, than himself. For there can be no experience of change even in the experienced so long as it remains absolutely undifferentiated from the Experiencer who, remaining *what he is,* realises it as an inseparable aspect of himself. The super-imposition, therefore, is possible only when the Experiencer comes to identify himself in feeling with the experienced, *after* it has once been already perceived as *not*-himself,—at least to a certain degree, as it is in the Shuddha Vidyā State. By this identification only can Māyā infect the Experiencer with

1. Jñāna sometimes means also limited knowledge in the Trika. Comp. ज्ञानं बन्धः; *Shiv. Sū.*, i. 2.

the changes of the Experienced. That this is the way of Māyā or the Force of Obscuration can also be seen in the experiences of our daily life. So long as what is vaguely called a man's 'spirit' maintains itself in a state of feeling—no matter whether it is consciously realised or is working as a sub-conscious element of experience—which makes the 'spirit' realise itself as *superior* to, and above and beyond, what is generally and equally vaguely termed the 'flesh', one seldom feels sleepy even when the 'flesh' is very weary. But the moment this feeling is gone and the 'spirit', as it were, succumbs to the weight and influence of the 'flesh' and becomes as it were one with the latter, instead of remaining a thing which is above and beyond it, that is, instead of remaining in a state of elation, it is overtaken by the weariness of the 'flesh' and the man feels tired and becomes drowsy.

This being the way of the Force of Obscuration in any of its forms, Māyā first leads the Experiencer to feel himself as one with the Experienced,[1] which has already once been realised as something other than himself, *i. e.*, as the 'not-Self,'—as is the case partially at least in the previously produced Suddha Vidyā state,—*before* she can fully bring on that sense of Obscuration which results in the above mentioned change in the fivefold relation of the Experiencer—a change which is due to that taking place really in the other term of the relation, namely, the Experienced. In other words, before this change in the relation takes place, the Self of the Experience becomes, as it were, one with its not-Self, which the Experienced at this stage is, and is thereby infected with the defects of the latter.

And the moment the Self becomes identified with the not-Self, the five typical forms of perfect relation mentioned above also become defective—they become imper-

---

1. स मेयः सन्; *Īsh. Prat.*, III. i. 9.

fect and limited. They change, as also said above, respectively into the vague experiences of

1. Change in the Experiencer himself *i. e.* of Time which is the same thing as the experience of change (Kāla);
2. Confinement to a limited location and therefore restricted access and Regulation as to cause, sequence, occasion and the like (Niyati); [1].
3. Limited Interest so as to find oneself attending to one or a few things at a time (Rāga);
4. Limited Consciousness (Vidyā);

and 5. Limited Authorship—(Kalā)[2].

And the way these changes in the Experiencer are produced by the operation of Māyā is something like the following:—

The Experiencer, after he has for a time 'gazed' at and enjoyed the grandeur of the 'All-this,' feels as it were 'proud' of it, and becomes 'immersed' in the thought: 'All-this' is mine; I am the author of 'All-this.' As this thought grows in strength, the Experiencer becomes entirely 'absorbed' in it and with the absorbtion comes a feeling of identification, as it may to any of us in our daily lives, when thinking too much of a thing as 'I' and 'mine'.

With absorption, and therefore with identification thus produced by Māyā, the Experiencer loses the realisation of 'himself' *as* the Self of the Experience; and as this happens he becomes sleepy .[3]

---

1. Niyati also leads to the experience of Desha or space, *i. e.*, the experience of spatial or positional relations.

2. The order given here of the five Kañchukas or Limitations is that of Utpalāchārya (see *Vṛitti* on *Īsh. Prat.*, III. i. 9). Abhinava Gupta counts them in the following order:—Kalā, Vidyā, Rāga, Kāla and Niyati.

3. Comp. सुप्तस्थानीयमणुम् ; *Tantrasāra*, Ahn. 8.

As the Experiencer falls asleep, the perception of the 'All-this' itself, in which he had himself been at first lost, grows dim. It then is realised not as a clear and clearly defined 'All-this,' but as a *vague, indistinct and undefined something* which is practically the same as 'Nothing' (Shūnya[1]), not unlike the 'nothing' of the experience of the really dreamless deep-sleep state in our daily life.

With this change in the Experiencer :—

1. What was Nityatva becomes Kāla as the Experiencer formulates in thought, however indistinctly, the *new* experience, and, as it were, says to himself: "I *was erstwhile* enjoying All-this and *now* I *am* feeling but a dim shadow of it." Needless to say there is in this experience scarcely a clear realisation of the 'I', such as would be necessary if the experience of this state were really expressed in words. It is only a *dim* experience of the *change* and therefore of *Time*; and it *would* be expressed in the way stated above only if the realisation of the 'I' were as distinct as it is in the ordinary waking consciousness of daily life, or, better still, in the Shuddha Vidyā stage described previously.

2. Vyāpakatva changes into Niyati as the Experiencer is *constrained* to the dim perception of the vague '*some*-this'—and nothing else—as an inevitable sequence of the previously realised '*All*–this'.

3. Pūrṇatva is reduced to Rāga as the Interest in the universal 'All–this' flags, overtaken by the sleep of Māyā as the Experiencer now is.

---

1. This should throw some light on the Buddhist doctrine of the 'Shūnya' which, though a 'Nothing,' is still regarded as a reality.

4. Sarvajñatva becomes only Vidyā, perceiving only a limited something—a dim, vague and undefined 'Something' which is as good as Nothing.

And 5. Sarvakartṛitva assumes the form of Kalā as the drowsy Being feels *how little* he is now capable of accomplishing.

Thus when, after the appearance of the Shuddha Vidyā, Māyā, the Obscuring Force, comes into play, she brings into existence, along with her, (or, more correctly perhaps, as her progeny) five other forms of Limitation. And with these she enwraps the Experiencer—as a baby with swaddling clothes—who thereby becomes oblivious of his true Divine State; and, forgetting his own glory, falls as it were into a sleep in which he has but a vague notion of experiencing an equally vague, indistinct and undefined 'Something' into which the glorious 'All-this' of the previous state has now been reduced.

Two Principles of Limited Individual Subject-Object

The Purusha

This Experiencer, thus put into sleep by Māyā, who has hidden away from him his own Divine State and Glory, and has besides fully restrained him by wrapping round him the swaddling clothes of the five limitations of Kāla, Niyati, Rāga, Vidyā and Kalā, and thus vaguely feeling an equally vague and indefinite 'Something' as the content of his experience—this Experiencer in this state of experience is technically called Purusha, which we may translate as the limited Individual Spirit, or simply Spirit, (lit. Man; hence to be referred to as *he*).

And it is produced, let me repeat, by the operation of Māyā in the way indicated above, *after* the manifestation of the Shuddha Vidyā.

And as, in order to bring the Purusha into existence, Māyā *wraps* him up both in herself and in the other five forms of limitation, these together with herself are called the six Kañchukas *i. e.* sheaths, cloaks or swaddling clothes of the Spirit.

And while Māyā, together with the five other Kañchukas, makes the existence of the limited Individual Spirit as such—*i. e.* of the Puruṣha—possible, the Puruṣha himself and in reality is only the Divine Experiencer who becomes thus limited by allowing himself to be enwrapped and enshrouded by Māyā and her progeny, but yet without undergoing any *real* change in himself inasmuch as he still remains as he ever was, not only in the Shuddha Vidyā stage but also in the other forms which come into existence previous to the manifestations of the latter, and, ultimately, as it were, behind and beyond them all and yet pervading them all, as Parama Shiva, or Parā Saṁvit, the Supremest Experience. That is to say the All-experiencer becomes the Puruṣha, to use the technical language of the system, following the Ābhāsa process which leaves entirely unaffected the primary as well as each successively originating source, even when products come into manifestation.

Not only this; when the process reaches the stage in which the Puruṣha comes into manifestation, something more also happens. For when the Puruṣha comes into being, by means of the Ābhāsa process, the All-Experiencer is thereby not only not affected in any way and remains the same as he ever was, but he goes on producing such Puruṣhas and multiplying their number indefinitely; that is to say, he goes on apparently dividing and expanding himself to an indefinite extent, without ever showing the slightest sign of exhaustion and diminution.

In other words, the All-Experiencer, while remaining ever the same, produces, by the Ābhāsa process, not only a single Puruṣha, but, by repeating the same process, becomes, *i. e.* experiences himself as, an endless number of such Puruṣhas who realise themselves as all differentiated, and even separated, from one another, as, let us say, a number of living cells may experience themselves as distinct and even separated from one another even though they may be, indeed are, produced and differentiated from a single source of life; or, as the various 'personalities' 'dissociated' *i. e.* differentiated from a single 'personality'—namely, the one 'subliminal self,'—may realise themselves as mutually distinct and even as independent of each other; or, even as the ultimate units of matter—by whatever name they may finally come to be known, electrons, ions or otherwise—may come to exist as mutually exclusive entities from an all-filling single source, by a process of apparent division which still leaves that source all unaffected[1].

This happens just because the All-Experiencer remains what he has ever been even when a Puruṣha is produced. And remaining *always* what he is in his aspect as *himself*, in another aspect he also *constantly* falls asleep; that is to say, he is falling asleep, or, is assuming a limited aspect, every successive moment of time. [That is, as it would appear to us limited Experiencers. There are really no moments of time from the standpoint of the all-experiencer but only that Eternity which is beyond all time conceived as an aggregate, *i. e.* as a measureless succession, of moments. See note 2, page 61 *ante*.] But while the aspect in which he ever remains *himself* is and must be one and the same, the 'sleeping' or the limited aspect he assumes every moment of time cannot be so. That is to say, while he is always one and the same in his aspect

---

1. This process of multiplication or differentiation is really only another phase of the operation of Māyā which not only obscures but also divides or re-duplicates by first obscuring the reality. Comp. the following:—

मायाविभेदबुद्धिर्निजांशजातेषु निखिलभावेषु ।
नित्यं तस्य निरङ्कुशविभवं वेलेव वारिधे रुन्धे ॥ *Tattva Sand.*, 5.

as himself, what he assumes as a 'sleeping' or limited aspect every moment of time is a fresh or a new one; and he thus produces as many separate aspects as there are moments of time. That is to say, he produces an infinite *i. e.* unlimited number of aspects which are none other than the unlimited number of Puruṣhas which constitute the aggregate of individual Spirits, actual or possible, in the Universe.

This happens at this stage, and *not* in the previous stages of the Pure Order—even though in those stages also the source from which the products come into manifestation remains ever the same and unaffected in itself—because in those stages there enters no element of limitation of the *kind* produced by Māyā. There the products are universal and unlimited as to time, space, form or characteristics; and as such none of them could be a manifold in the sense of having mutually exclusive limitation.

There indeed is a *sort* of manyness even in the various stages of the Pure Order as will be seen later. But for all practical purposes the experiencing entity in each of the stages of that Order is a unity. For if there be more than one Experiencer in any one of those stages, they are all so alike in all respects and so much identified with one another as to the content of experience, equally experiencing the whole of the Experienced,—the 'All-this' and the 'This' of the Ideal Universe respectively in the Sad Vidyā and the Aishvara stages—or equally realising themselves as the pure Being of the Sādākhya and as the pure Bliss and the pure 'I' of the Shakti-Shiva stage, that they constitute in each of these stages practically a single and identical experiencing entity, without any one of them, in a particular stage, in any way whatsoever limiting or excluding the others belonging to the same stage. And if they are all identical in respect of the content of experience they are not limited by time or space either. There being no sort of *change* in their experience, so long as the particular stage in which they are manifest lasts, they are beyond all conditions of past, present and future; that is to say, they realise themselves as existing *eternally*, or, which is the same thing, in an alwaysness which bears the same relation to the flow of past, present and future, *i. e.* of time, as a mathematical point does to the various extensions and directions of positional relation *i. e.* of space. Similarly, from one point of view, they occupy *all–space*, being universally present everywhere, and from another, only what is a mathematical point.

Thus, multiplicity in the product, in the sense of limited and mutually exclusive manyness, begins only with the introduction of limitation *i. e.* with the operation of the Self-hiding Power or Force of Māyā, who or which is thus not only a power of 'obscuration' but, as said above, also one of multiplication and differentiation.

Further, and finally, as, by obscuration, limitation differentiation and multiplication, Māyā brings the Puruṣhas into existence, each of these numberless Puruṣhas becomes an Aṇu, a non-spatial point—almost like a mathematical point. For limitation of an omnipresent something which is itself non-spatial—as Parama Shiva is—cannot have any other meaning. It cannot be anything with a limited extension or with a 'middle measure' as it is technically called.[1]

The Prakriti and the Gunas

Simultaneously with the manifestation of the Puruṣha by the operation of Māyā, there is produced another very important result. It is already said that, 'sleeping' as he is, the Puruṣha still has the Experience of a vague and indefinite 'Something', which forms at this stage the

1. पूर्णत्वाभावेन परिमितत्वाद् अणुत्वम्; *Prat. Vṛit.*, III. ii. 4.

object—if such a term may be used in this connection—
of the Experience. Now, this vague, undefined and indefinite 'Something' is a factor which is not to be ignored.
For it can be nothing else than the Universal 'All-this'
now perceived through the influence of Māyā in this dim
and indefinite fashion; and as such it is the root and
source of all future experience. How it is so will be
shown presently. For the present we have just to recognise its presence in the Experience of the Puruṣha.
Indeed there can be no Puruṣha without it, so long as a
Puruṣha is under the influence of Māyā, as all Puruṣhas
are, till by a process to be explained later they can rise
above it, and thus practically cease to be Puruṣhas in the
sense of experiencing entities enwrapped in the Kañchukas. For a Puruṣha is only a limited form of the All-
Experiencer of the previous state; and as such it can no
more exist without its relations than the All-Experiencer
can. Relations there must be in the Puruṣha. Only these
relations in the case of the All-Experiencer of the previous state are of a universal nature, while in the
Puruṣha they become necessarily limited and completely
contracted. But however contracted, they can never be
relations unless there be, above and beyond the Puruṣha,
some other term or terms which they relate with the
Puruṣha. Thus for the existence of the Puruṣha as a
being with relations—which relations, let me repeat, are
essential to him for his very manifestation as Puruṣha—
it is necessary that there must be a *second term* to which
the Puruṣha is related. And this second term in this state
can be no other than the 'Indefinite Something' mentioned above. It is thus a most important factor—as important
as the Puruṣha himself. And it comes into manifestation
simultaneously with the Puruṣha. Indeed, if the Puruṣha
is only the All-Experiencer, put to sleep and 'cribbed,
cabined and confined,' this 'Indefinite Something' of the

experience at this stage is nothing but the Universal 'All-this' now dimly and vaguely perceived [1].

Coming into manifestation simultaneously with the Purusha, it is called his Prakṛiti—She who affects the Purusha or whom he has placed before him to be acted upon by and to react upon.

Thus the Purusha and the Prakṛiti are nothing but the limited representations of the two factors in the two-sided Experience of the Shuddha Vidyā state. And as the number of Purushas produced by the process described above is, as has been pointed out, unlimited and unending, similarly the Prakṛitis are also infinite in number, one for each Purusha, the one universal All-this being perceived dimly by the different Purushas as so many different 'this'es diversely reflected in the ocean of Māyā, as different persons may perceive the same sun as so many different reflections in different parts of the sea.[2]

---

1. एवं किञ्चित्कर्तृत्वं यन् मायाकार्यं, तत्र किंचित्त्वविशिष्टं यत् कर्तृत्वं विशेष्यं, तत्र व्याप्रियमाणा कला विद्यादिप्रसवहेतुरिति निरूपितम् । इदानीं विशेषणभागो यः किंचिदित्युक्तो ज्ञेयः कार्यश्च, तं यावत् सा कला स्वात्मनः पृथक् कुरुते तावदेष एव सुख-दुःख-मोहात्मक-भोग्यविशेषानुस्यूतस्य सामान्यमात्रस्य तद्गुणसाम्यापरनाम्नः प्रकृतितत्त्वस्य सर्गः—इति भोक्तृ-भोग्ययुगलस्य **सममेव** कलातत्त्वायत्ता सृष्टिः । *Tantrasāra*, Ahn. 8.

एवं कलाख्यतत्त्वस्य किञ्चित्कर्तृत्वलक्षणे ।
विशेष्यभागे कर्तृत्वं चर्चितं भोक्तृपूर्वकम् ॥
विशेषणतया योऽत्र किञ्चिद्भागस्तदुत्थितम् ।
वेद्यमात्रं स्फुटं भिन्नं प्रधानं सूयते कला ॥ *Tantrāl.*, Āhn. 9.

तच्च [प्रधानं] भिन्नं प्रतिपुंनियतत्वाद् अनेकम् इति यावत् । कलादीनां च तथात्वेऽपि स्फुटं, तदपेक्षया स्थूलमित्यर्थः; *Viveka* on above.

सममेव हि भोग्यं च भोक्तारं च प्रसूयते ।
कला भेदाभिसंधानादवियुक्तं परस्परम् ॥
एवं संवेद्यमात्रं यत् सुख-दुःख-विमोहतः ।
भोत्स्यते यत्ततः प्रोक्तं तत्साम्यात्मकमादितः ॥ *Tantrāl.* Āhn. 9.

2. Note this fundamental difference between the Trika and the Sāṅkhya conceptions of the Prakṛiti. The Sāṅkhya Prakṛiti is one and universal for all and thus corresponds in this respect to the Māyā of the Trika. See also note 1 above, and Appendix V.

The Experience of his Prakṛiti, on the part of a Purusha, is one in which, while there is no movement whatever of thought or activity,—it being a state, as it were, of sleep,—there is no *specific feeling* of any sort either. That is to say, it is a state in which the Experienced does not produce in the Experiencer either that calm feeling of mere presentation or mere awareness in which the Experiencer remains blissfully motionless, *calmly* enjoying what is before him; or that disquieting feeling of excitement or interest which *moves* him forth into activity of some sort; or even that feeling of dulling callousness and stupefaction to which one quite *inertly* submits. It is therefore a state of Equipoise,—Equipoise, namely, between the calm and *peaceful* feeling of pleasing but unmoving awareness, pure and simple, the *active* feeling of a *moving* interest and the *passive* and *inert* feeling of stupefaction—Feelings or Affections for which the *technical* Sanskrit names are respectively Sukha, Duḥkha and Moha (literally, Pleasure, Pain and Delusion or Bewilderment).

And this is so, because there is no *one* element or *feature* which is *more* prominent, rather more prominently manifest, than others in the Prakṛiti—it being merely a vague and undefined 'Something' in which all the distinguishing features of the various content of the Universal 'All-this' are obliterated—so that there can be nothing *standing out* which can induce any of these feelings in the Experiencer. The Experience of Prakṛiti, therefore, being an equipoise of the three Feelings, of calm, peaceful and blissful Awareness, of moving Interest and Passion, and of dull and callous Stupefaction, Prakṛiti herself, that is the indefinite and undefined 'Something' itself of the experience at this stage, is and must be a thing in which all Elements or Features capable of inducing, or *affecting us*, these three Feelings are held in a state of Equipoise.

Now, the Elements or Features which can induce the three Feelings of calm *Awareness*, moving *Passion* and dulling *Stupefaction* (of Sukha, Duḥkha and Moha, as they are *technically* called in Sanskrit) are and must be themselves only three, corresponding to the number of the feelings they can produce in an individual—feelings which are essentially different from one another and of which there are no more than the three named above. They are called in Sanskrit the Sattva, the Rajas and the Tamas, (producing respectively Sukha, Duḥkha and Moha)—terms which must be retained untranslated, because there are no single words in English that can adequately render all that these technical names imply; for they are *not only* the originators of the above named Feelings *but also a great deal more* as will be seen later. Collectively they are called the three Guṇas, meaning literally the three Threads, as of a chord, or three Factors, Attributes or Features.

And as, in the Prakṛiti, all Feeling-inducing or Affective Features are held in a State of equipoise, Prakṛiti is, speaking technically, only the equipoise of the three Guṇas of Sattva, Rajas, and Tamas[1].

And as there is on the part of a Purusha, no specific experience in his Prakṛiti, but only a general *feeling* of a vague and indefinite something, Prakṛiti is called 'the generally-experienced (bhogya-sāmānya).' [1]

From Prakṛiti, as 'the generally experienced,' is produced *everything* of specific experiences, which the limited Individual Spirit or the Purusha can ever have, whether as objects or as the means whereby such objects are experienced.

And the process following which these means and objects of experience come into manifestation is much the same as has been recognised by the Sāṅkhya system.

---

1. Comp. तदेव [प्रकृतितत्त्वं] तु भोग्यसामान्यं प्रक्षोभगतं गुणातत्त्वम्; *Tantrasāra*, Āhn. 8.

There are slight differences of course, but it is substantially the same process. One of the reasons why there are any differences between the teachings of the two systems is perhaps to be found in the fact that, while the Shaiva system makes a clear distinction between the Universal, or the Pure and Perfect, and the limited Individual, that is, the Impure and Imperfect processes, the Sāṅkhya—*i. e.* the Sāṅkhya as represented by the Kārikās of Īshvara Kṛiṣhṇa, the commentary on the Tattva-Samāsa and apparently also the Sāṅkhya Sūtras, which is a much later work, but *not* the Sāṅkhya of the Purāṇas—makes no such distinction At least this distinction is not apparent from the above named main Texts on the subject, even though Vijñāna Bhikṣhu seeks to establish it by regarding the process from a two-fold point of view, *viz.*, the Samaṣhṭi and the Vyaṣhṭi *i. e.* Collective and Distributive, as indeed it can be and is so regarded even by the Trika, as will be seen later. However this may be, the process of manifestation from now on, as recognised by the Trika, is practically the same as that described in the Sāṅkhya. We may therefore try to understand it in the light of the latter system. Indeed, our understanding of it will be greatly facilitated by a reference to the Sāṅkhya.

Now, Puruṣha and Prakṛiti come into manifestation, as said above, by the All-Experiencer assuming, as it were, a sleeping aspect. In that state the All-Experiencer has no clear notion of the 'All-this' but only feels it as a mere 'Something,' which is entirely vague, indefinite and undefined. Nor does he realise *himself* with any better or greater clearness as the 'I' of the Experience. Indeed its self-realisation as the 'I' is as vague as its realisation of the 'Something' of the Experience, and may be likened to the realisation of the 'I' in the deep and really dreamless sleep of our individual experience. *And it is a point which should be clearly noted.*

Principles of Mental Operation:

Buddhi, Ahaṅkāra, and Manas

This being the experience of the Purusha-Prakṛiti state, the manifestation which follows next is, *in one respect at least*, not unlike the experience we sometimes have immediately on waking[1]. It is technically called, as in the Sāṅkhya, the Buddhi, which term may perhaps be translated as Consciousness-as-such, but which, like so many others, must be left untranslated. We shall only explain what it means. For a clear comprehension, however, of what Buddhi really is, we have to consider it along with two other factors the manifestation of which follows that of the Buddhi. These are technically called Ahaṅkāra and Manas, of which the one may perhaps be translated as the Personal Consciousness, Personal Ego or Self-apperception and the other as Imagination (which however is only *one* of the functions of Manas).

Now, to understand what these three, Buddhi, Ahaṅkāra and Manas—or, as we shall take them here in their reverse order, Manas, Ahaṅkāra and Buddhi—really are, we must make an analysis of the psychical process which is daily and hourly going on in us.

When we perceive a thing and *think* or *speak* of it, saying ' it is so and so '—it is a cow, for instance—our experience of this perception of a cow *as expressed* in words or *expressible*, i. e., *conceived* or *thought of*, involves a complicated process which consists of *at least four*[2] clearly defined operations, even though they may not always be *realised* as thus defined at the time one has the experience, not only on account of the great swiftness with which these operations are gone through, but also because of their simultaneousness which is not unoften the case. They may be stated as follows :—

---

1. Comp. सुप्तोत्थितचित्तवत्; *Yoga-Vārttika* on ii. 19.

2. I say *at least four*, because the Trika recognises several more not recognised by the Sāṅkhya and others.

The first operation is that of the senses,—sensation as it is called; (Ālochana in Sanskrit[1]). In this very first operation there is involved another, namely, that of what may be called Attention, without the *co*-operation of which there can be no sensation at all,—as is known to all from experience,—even when what are called the objects of sense perception are in relation with the senses. But, apart from this operation of the 'Attention'—which operation may be considered as practically one with that of the senses, inasmuch as the latter can never work without it, and which therefore need not be separately noted here for our present purpose, although we shall have to take it into consideration later on—there is another operation, which as it were builds up, or rather carves, the image of the object to be perceived and thought of, out of the whole blocks of sensations which are, at the time, pressing upon the experiencing subject from all sides. This operation consists in 'desiring'[2] *i. e.* seeking for and '*selecting*'[3] a certain group, to the *exclusion*[3] of others, out of the confused and confusing heap, with a view to or with the *intention* of, making a *particular* image or a *particular object of consciousness* with this speci-

---

1. रूपादिषु पञ्चानाम् **आलोचन**मात्रमिष्यते वृत्तिः । *Sāṅkh. Kār.* 28.

What is given by sensation or Ālochana is absolutely unspeakable *i. e.* uncommunicable to others, as it consists of an absolute particularity. Hence it is said that it is

'बालमूकादिविज्ञानसदृशम्मुग्धवस्तुजम्'; *Tattva-kau.* on the above.

2. एषणा or संकल्प; *Tantrāloka*, Ahn. ix. See *infra*. For the various meanings of संकल्प see also Appendix **VI.**

3. व्यवच्छेद or भेद. See *infra* p. 99 note 2, the passage quoted from the *Tantrāloka* where the function of Manas is described as व्यवच्छेद. First there is व्यवच्छेद by Manas, and then the व्यवच्छिन्न is assimilated (अभिमत) by Ahaṅkāra. Nârâyaṇa (*Sāṅkh. Chan.* 29.) speaks of the function of manas as भेदक,—'मनसः [स्वालक्षण्यं] सविकल्पकं संकल्पापरपर्यायं भेदकम् इत्यर्थः ।'

Vāchaspati Mishra (*Tattva-kau.* 27) also speaks of the function of Manas as व्यवच्छेद,—'व्यवच्छिन्दन् मनो लक्षयति.'

ally marked out group.[1] Thus, for instance, as I am perceiving my cow, I am having, crowding upon me, a whole host of other sensations as well—those affecting me as the surrounding scenery, the blue of the sky, the green of the meadow, the singing of birds and so on. These are all being *left out* and only those affecting me as the cow are being sought and singled out and built into the image of the cow.

This 'desiring for,' this seeking and singling out a certain special group from among a whole crowd of sensations with the intention of building up, with the selected group, the image of an object (or, which is the same thing, the object itself)—this is an operation which is quite other than and different from the first operation of mere sensation. It is the *second* operation in the process leading to the perception of my cow so as to be able to think and speak of it. It is what may be called the 'Image-making' or Imaginative Operation—the operation, in this instance, of imaging forth the cow with the ingredients of a *particular* group of sensations 'desired for' *i. e.* sought and selected out of a whole mass of them.[2]

It is an operation of image-making from another point of view also—I mean the standpoint of modern Western Psychology. For, according to the findings of that Psychology, the process of sensation consists in receiving by the senses not a completed picture extended in space, as, for instance, the colour or colours of our cow, like so many *patches* stretched out in space, but like so many *points* of that colour or those colours. The senses give us what is technically called a manifold—the manifold of the sense.

---

1. मनः............सामान्यत इन्द्रियेण गृहीतमर्थं सम्यक् कल्पयति......इति विशिष्टधीजनकम् । *Sāṅkh. Chan.* 27.

2. यदा प्रार्थयते किञ्चित् तदा भवति सा मनः । *Mahābhārata*, xii. 247. 9. See Appendix V. (Chap. 254 of Kumbakonam edition).

Now, in order that these colour-points may be made into *a whole*—a whole patch or patches of colours—assuming a particular shape and form, namely, that of a particular cow, there must be a *second* operation in the psychical process by which, these 'points of sensation,' the manifold of the sense, are gathered together and made into such a whole of a particular shape and form—in other words, into a picture or *image.*

However that may be, the image-making constituting the second operation in the psychical process would not alone enable me to speak or think of the object of my present perception as a cow. For what I am actually perceiving, *i. e.*, the actually given of the sense, is no more than a *mere* colour-form (supposing I am only *seeing* the cow but not hearing it make a sound or produce any other sensation in me, in which case the imaginative operation would include also a synthesising or concreting process to be noticed later) which is stretched out in space assuming a particular shape either moving or stationary. To transform this mere picture, which is hardly better than one on canvas, or than that of a cinematograph show, it must be endowed with various other properties as well, solidity, life and so on. Now these properties the sense now in operation, *viz.*, that of sight, is not perceiving when it is revealing to me the cow's presence as a patch of colour or colours stretched out in space. They are supplied from *somewhere else*, namely, from the memory of my *personal* experience of the past, stored up in *myself* as a *particular individual* or *person*, i. e., out of myself. There is *absolutely* no other source but *myself* from which they can be supplied. Nor can the elements supplied be anything else but a part of my *own personal self* as built up by and with elements supplied out of experiences I have had as a *particular person* born and brought up in a particular situation or situations. That is to say, before my mere colour-form, carved out of the block of mere sensations, can be transformed into the live object I am thinking of as my cow, it has to be endowed with something of *myself.*

Not only this. It has to be *assimilated to* and *identified with* [1] what is in myself as a particular person. For how can I think or speak of the present object as 'cow' unless I realise it as something *similar* to such an experience of my own in the past—an experience which is now part of myself? Again, how can this assimilation and identification be possible unless and until the new experience be taken up into *myself*—brought into the midst of what is *me* and *mine*? Thus not only must the mere image be endowed with a part of myself, before it can be perceived and thought of as my cow, but the image itself will also have to be brought into me—*into my own self.* That is to say, to use the somewhat dry language of philosophy, it has to be referred to what is already me and mine.

It is this endowing of the sensation-image with part of myself and *assimilating* it to what is already in *me*, which constitutes the *third operation* in the psychical process giving me the perception of my cow.

But even this operation does not quite give me my cow, so as to be able to think and speak of it as a cow—saying ' What I see before me is *a cow* '.

For, before I can speak thus of the now assimilated image, I must not only make a comparison with other

---

1. अभिमत; *Tantrāloka*, Āhn. 9. See *infra* passage quoted. अभिमानोऽहङ्कारः; *Sāṅkh. kār.* 24. Abhimāna means 'identification' in thought and feeling; also assimilation, and appropriation or self-arrogation. All other meanings, such as pride, vanity and the like are derived from this primary meaning. There can be no pride or arrogance in regard to anything unless the same is thought of and felt as one's own, as belonging to oneself

cows I have seen and known in the past as my *personal* experiences, but also refer it to the *species* cow. Till this is done I can never speak of the image which is being perceived as *a cow*, which statement only means that it is *one* of a *species* called cow. But whence do we get this idea of a Species? I have never experienced such a thing as cow as a Species as one of my *personal* experiences—I have known only particular and individual cows. There must therefore be in me *a standard of reference* which has this experience of the Species; and it must be *impersonal* in the sense that its contents as such—*i. e.* as abstract or general ideas such as that of a species, of triangularity for instance—cannot be pictured by the *individual mind* of a *person* such as a Rāma or a Jones, in the same way as a particular thing or act can; and therefore it must be beyond the range of *personal* experiences which any of us as Rāma or Shyāma, as John or Jones, may have had in the past.[1] It is only by referring to this standard that we are able to form a judgment such as—"It is a cow".

This reference to such a standard is the *fourth* operation in our experience of thinking and speaking of an object of perception as 'such and such a thing and *not* such and such another thing'—'as a cow and not as a horse or dog'.[2]

---

1. See the next note however.

2. अध्यवसायो बुद्धिः। सोऽयमध्यवसायो गवादिषु यस्मात् प्रतिपत्तिः 'एवमेतन् नान्यथा'। 'गौरवे अयं, नाश्वः'; 'स्थाणुरेव अयं, न पुरुषः' इत्येषा निश्चयात्मिका बुद्धिः। *Tattva-Samāsa.*

Although beyond the actual realisation by the consciousness of the individual *as* Rāma or Jones, Buddhi, from the Trika point of view, is not entirely unknown. Only it cannot be pictured to one's limited personal consciousness in the same way as a concrete thing can. Compare the following:—

ननु असंविदितं तावत् करणं न स्यात्; बुद्धिश्च मनोऽहंकारवत् न संवेद्या इति कथमस्याः करणत्वं युज्यते इत्याशंक्य आह—

Now, of these operations, the first is, as is obvious, the one which is carried on by means of what are called the senses—*they* are the *means* of gaining experience in so far as this first operation is concerned.

Corresponding to these means of the first operation, there are and must be for the other operations also what act as such *means*. And it is these *means* of the three subsequent psychic operations which are respectively called the Manas, the Ahaṅkāra and the Buddhi.[1]

न च बुद्धिरसंवेद्या करणत्वान्मनो यथा ।
प्रधानवदसंवेद्यबुद्धिवादस्तदुज्झितः ॥

'असंवेद्यबुद्धिवाद' इति सांख्याभ्युपगतः । अयं च अत्र प्रयोगः—बुद्धिः संवेद्या, करणत्वात् । यत् करणं तत् संवेद्यं, यथा मनः । यन् न संवेद्यं तन् न करणं, यथा प्रधानम् । बुद्धिश्च करणम् । तस्मात् संवेद्येति । संवेद्यत्वे च अस्या गुणान्वितत्वं हेतुः प्रधानेनानैकान्तिक इति ।

तुल्ये गुणान्वितत्वे तु संवेद्यं चित्तमिष्यते ।
बुद्धिश्चापि ह्यसंवेद्या धन्या तार्किकता तव ॥

इत्याद्युपेक्ष्यम् ॥ *Tantrāl.* with *Viv.*, Āhn. 9.

For a discussion from the Hindu point of view of the old, old question whether there are any general ideas at all, apart from and other than those gradually built up by our personal experiences, in the same way as the ideas of the concrete are built up, see Appendix VII.

1. On the whole of the above comp., among others, the following:—

तत्र पृथिव्याद्याभासा एव मिश्रीभूय घटादिस्वलक्षणीभूताः कर्मेन्द्रियैः उपसर्पिताः, बुद्धीन्द्रियैः आलोचिताः, **अन्तःकरणेन संकल्पिताः**, अभिमतनिश्चितरूपया विद्यया विवेचिताः, कलादिभिः अनुरञ्जिताः, प्रमातरि विश्राम्यन्ति ॥ *Prat. Vim.*, III. i. 12.

बुद्ध्यहंकृन्मनः प्राहुर्बोध-संरम्भणेषणे ।
करणं बाह्यदेवैर्यन् नैवाप्यन्तर्मुखैः कृतम् ॥

बोधः शब्दादेर्विषयस्य अध्यवसायः । संरम्भः अहमात्माभिमानः । एषणम् इच्छा, संकल्पः ॥ *Tantrāloka*, Āhn. ix, with comm.

अवसायोऽभिमानश्च कल्पनं चेति न क्रिया ।
एकरूपा; ततस्त्रित्वं युक्तमन्तःकृतौ स्फुटम् ॥

न एकरूपेति,—स्यति-मन्यति-क्लृप्तीनां भिन्नत्वात्, (i) अन्यव्यवच्छेदेन (ii) अभिमतस्य (iii) अवसायो हि एषामेकविषयत्वेऽपि विभिन्नं कार्यं भवेदिति भावः; तदुक्तम्

Manas is what 'desires' *i. e.*, seeks for and singles out a particular group of sensations from among a whole crowd of them, and builds up particular images therewith; or, to use a different metaphor, carves an image out of a whole block of sensations given by the senses at the time. From another point of view it is what synthesises the discrete manifold of the senses, and builds up 'mental images' of them.

Ahaṅkāra is what gathers and stores up the memory of *personal* experiences, and 'identifies' and 'assimilates' the experiences of the present, of which experiences the sum total, thus held together by it, constitutes what we realise as our *personal* 'Ego'—as the individual and particular 'I' of the every day life of limited experiencers, such as human beings ordinarily are. For, in so far as this 'I' is *personal* and *peculiar* to a man as Rāma or Jones, —in so far as it is nothing but this—it is only an *aggregate* of these personal experiences either as memories or as actualities regarded as oneself. Ahaṅkāra is, in other words, what makes the 'artificial' or 'made up' 'I' of an individual, as distinguished from the real and innermost 'I', which every one is as Parama Shiva. The artificial 'I' is only produced by the identification with and

---

क्लृप्तिर्मतिः स्यतिश्चैव जाता भिन्नार्थवाचकाः ।
इच्छा संरम्भ-बोधार्थास्तेनान्तःकरणं त्रिधा ॥ *Ibid.*

And also:

अस्ति ह्यालोचनं ज्ञानं प्रथमं निर्विकल्पकम् ।
... ... ॥
ततः परं पुनर्वस्तु धर्मैर्जात्यादिभिर्यया ।
बुद्ध्याऽवसीयते ... ... ॥

Quoted by Vāchaspati Mishra on *Shāṅkh. Kār.* 27, and by Vijñānabhikṣhu on *Sāṅkh. Sū.*, II. 32, and also by Aniruddha on *Ibid.*, I. 89., with variations.

assimilation to the real Self of the now produced not-self.[1]

Finally 'Buddhi' is that which, holding in it such *general ideas* as do not form the direct object of experience as concrete facts,—facts which one can definitely picture to oneself, like, for instance, the mental image of a particular cow or that of the performance of a particular act of kindness, ideas, in other words, which lie in the back-ground of, and are thus beyond, the 'personal Ego' *i. e.* the Ahaṅkāra—not only supplies that standard of reference which is needed for the formation of judgment, but also serves as the means whereby concrete experiences are, as it were, taken up unto itself for such reference and comparison. Buddhi may thus be spoken of as the *impersonal* or *superpersonal* state of consciousness, or experience in a limited individual (still *as* limited)[2].

---

1 "………अहंकारो येन बुद्धिप्रतिबिम्बिते वेद्यसंपर्के कलुषे पुंप्रकाशे अनात्मनि आत्माभिमानः शुक्तौ रजताभिमानवत्। अत एव 'कार' इत्यनेन कृतकत्वम् अस्य उक्तम्। सांख्यस्य तु तन्न युज्यते, स हि न आत्मनः अहंविमर्शमयतामिच्छति; वयं तु कर्तृत्वमपि तस्य इच्छामः। तच्च [*i. e.* कर्तृत्वं] शुद्धं विमर्श एव स्वात्मचमत्काररूपोऽहमिति।

Tantrasarā, Āhn. 8.

2. It is perhaps this state of super-personal experience, this Buddhi of the Hindu philosopher, which, at least in some of its aspects, is now being recognised in the West, by what has sometimes been called 'Abnormal Psychology,' as the subconscious or sub-liminal self of a man.

That such a state exists, indeed that all the states and their respective means or instruments mentioned above exist, in the depth of a man's being, can be ascertained, apart from all reasoning, by direct experience, if we are to believe the Hindu Philosophers, at least those of them who have, in addition to theoretical knowledge, practical experience as well *i. e.* the Yogins of the right kind, (not those distorters and torturers of the body and performers of juggling, hypnotising and such like feats for the delectation of the

But though super-personal, Buddhi is not entirely or absolutely inconceivable. We all of us probably have often had an experience which may, as hinted at above, give us an idea as to what the experience of Buddhi may

---

public, who also have come to be known by the name of Yogins, specially to the Western tourist) and who repeatedly assert the possibility and truth of such a direct experience. While the Yogins claim—they having trained their whole life, spiritual, mental, moral and physical, in a particular way—to be able to have this experience at will, others, even in the West, would seem to have had it as occasional glimpses over which they have little control. There is the remarkable example of Tennyson who, it is reported in one of the volumes of the *Nineteenth Century*, would rise to a state of consciousness in which he would feel as though all that constituted his personal 'I' *as Tennyson* had entirely vanished and would realise himself as above all such personality. He would get into this state, it is also reported, while slowly and mentally repeating to himself his own name—a remarkable practice which was very similar to the repetition on the part of the Yogins of particular words, or syllables of words, and of which *one* of the objects is said by the Yogins to be that, while it keeps one in a state of wakefulness, it also brings on a state of perfect peace and quiet resulting from the rythmic movement of the repetition. For the whole secret of Yoga, which is held to be the means of gaining the direct and first-hand experience of super-sensible realities, at first reasoned out or even learnt merely on faith as philosophic or religious truths, is that while the consciousness must be maintained at the very highest pitch of keen and tense attention, free from all feeling of dullness or sleepiness, it must also be absolutely free from all disturbance and movement caused by an uncontrolled passion, a feeling of anger or of hate or a curious interest, or even by an unmastered bodily condition. (See *Hindu Realism* pp. 142–148.) However this may be, that Tennyson would occasionally experience, while slowly and mentally repeating his own name, a state of impersonal or super-personal consciousness, which was not unlike the Buddhi of the Hindu Philosophers, would seem to be clear.

be like,—*in so far only* as it is an experience in which there is no definite and clear realisation of the 'I' or personal 'Ego.' This is the experience which is sometimes had, when on waking up from a state of deep and profound sleep, a man opens his eyes and is conscious only of what just meets the senses, while yet he is quite oblivious of himself as an 'I'—as such and such a person. Buddhi is not unlike this experience, inasmuch as there is in the Buddhi no thought of the 'I' as yet, the latter having already been suppressed in the Puruṣha-Prakṛiti state when the Experiencer, as it were, fell asleep[1].

This Buddhi comes into manifestation from Prakṛiti, as the Experiencer, as it were, wakes up, following the same or a similar law or principle which we find in operation in our daily lives, as our consciousness passes from a state of sleep to one of wakefulness[2].

Now the reason why one wakes up from a state of deep and profound sleep is, as will be readily seen, some disturbance in the body—either something from outside affecting the body and bodily organs or some change arising in the internal condition of the body itself, say, its being *refreshed* with rest, that is to say, its being revivified with fresh life and vigour, things which mean nothing else but some change in the condition of the body itself. And this is so, because sleep itself is due to a change in the condition of the body—of the 'flesh'—with which the 'Spirit' finds itself identified in feeling and experience. There can be really no sleep to the Spirit. If it finds itself asleep, it is only because it identifies itself with the 'flesh' in feeling and experience. And it is only the sleepiness of the flesh which can at

1. See ante p. 81, Note 3.

2. सुप्तोत्थितचित्तवत्; *Yoga-Vārttika*, on ii. 19.

all affect it, and make it also fall asleep.[1] This being the condition of falling asleep,—this change in the condition of the body with which the Spirit is identified—the waking up from sleep also depends on some change in the bodily condition. And, as, following this law, the sleeping Experiencer of the Purusha-Prakṛiti state, wakes up into a new consciousness again, he does so only because there takes place some change, some *disturbance* (Kṣhobha) in the Prakṛiti which served the Experiencer in the Puruṣha-Prakṛiti state, as his body, and with which he had already identified himself in feeling and thus fell asleep.

It would be interesting to discuss here how this disturbance—this Kṣhobha, as it is technically called in Sanskrit—at all takes place in the Prakṛiti, which, being inert, cannot of itself move. But we cannot enter into this discussion here as it involves the consideration of various other questions which can be cleared up only as we go on. For the present, it will be enough to say that it is produced by the action or will of the Experiencing Entity which, or who, has for his experience all the separate Prakṛitis, of all the limited Puruṣhas, as a collective whole. Such an entity in regard to any Tattva is called its Lord (Tattvesha); and it is the Lord of the Prakṛiti Tattva who creates 'disturbance' in the Prakṛiti of an individual Puruṣha, so that he may wake up and start on the round of limited life, of mixed experience of pleasure and pain, and thereby realise his moral worth, his merits and demerits, to the fullest extent. For we must not forget that the Universe to-be comes into existence for a moral purpose the true nature of which we shall see later on. [2]

1. The real Yogins of India maintain that they as Spirits can be fully conscious, even when the body lies quite asleep, by dissociating themselves in thought and feeling from the latter.

2 See *infra*; and also *Hindu Realism* p. 124.

Leaving these questions for the present then, what we have to grasp here is that, according to the Trika, in order that a Purusha may wake up from his sleep of the Purusha-Prakṛiti state, his Prakṛiti has to be disturbed by an influence other than that of either the Purusha himself, who has already completely identified himself with the Prakṛiti and has indeed forgotten himself, or of the Prakṛiti itself which is inert. [1]

As the Purusha wakes up, this his first waking conciousness after the sleep in or of the Prakṛiti—the consciousness, which is hardly anything more than a feeling of the merest presentation,[2] without anything of the nature of a *moving* feeling in it—is what is called Buddhi.

And as the first manifestation of that type of conscious experience which follows a state of sleep, it is and can be, *at this stage and in so far as it is the product of the experiences of the higher states af manifestation*, only the memory of the experience of the state which preceded the state of sleep [the meaning of the qualification made here will be understood later]. Buddhi is, in other words, what may be called the *memory* of the Universal 'All-this' which formed the Experience of the Shuddha-Vidyā but afterwards changed into a dim and indefinite 'Something' in the Purusha-Prakṛiti stage. It is therefore the blossoming forth *anew* of that indefinite 'Something' *i. e.* of Prakṛiti.

---

1 तदेव तु भोग्यसामान्यं प्रक्षोभगतं गुणतत्त्वम्; यत्र सुखं भोग्यरूपप्रकाशः सत्त्वम्; दुःखं प्रकाशाप्रकाशान्दोलनात्मकम् अत एव क्रियारूपं रजः; मोहः प्रकाशाभावरूपस्तमः। एवं **क्षुब्धात्** प्रधानात् कर्तव्यान्तरोदयः, **न अक्षुब्धात् । क्षोभः अवश्यमेव अन्तराले अभ्युपगन्तव्यः**।—इति सिद्धं सांख्यापरिदृष्टं पृथग्भूतं गुणतत्त्वम्। स च क्षोभः प्रकृतेः तत्त्वेशाधिष्ठानादेव। अन्यथा नियतं पुरुषं प्रति न सिध्येत्। *Tantrasāra*, Āhm. 8.

2 सत्तामात्रम्; see below. Comp. also सत्तामात्रे महति आत्मनि; Yoga-Bhāṣhya on ii. 19. See also the Vārttika on it.

As such, it is a state of calm but keenly *conscious* enjoyment, without as yet the manifestation of anything of the nature of either a moving Passion or inert, senseless Stupefaction. It is therefore the manifestation of the Sattva aspect of Prakṛiti as its *most dominant* Feature or Guṇa. Because a disturbance of the Prakṛiti, by which disturbance alone the new experience of Buddhi is produced, can mean nothing else than (*a*) that the equipoise in which the three Guṇas had hitherto been held, and which alone is the sole being and essence of the Prakṛiti, has been destroyed ; (*b*) that one or other of the three Guṇas which had been hitherto held in a state of mutual neutralisation has been thrown into greater prominence than the others ; and (*c*) that it is this prominent Feature thus produced which affects the Experiencer in a way which is other than the merely indefinite vague feeling of the Purusha-Prakṛiti State. That is to say, Buddhi is the 'affection' of the Purusha, as the *blissful* but *unmoving* feeling of *mere presentation* (prakāsha only), by the Prakṛiti in that Affective Feature (Guṇa) of hers which can so affect (*i. e.* in her aspect as the Sattva Guṇa), and which becomes, at the time, more prominent than her other two Features or aspects, both of which are also present therein but held in comparative suppression. [1]

And as the Buddhi, being such a manifestation of the Sattva Guṇa, is a glorious *vision* of ideas, (Dhī) *i. e.* the memory of the ' All-this ' at this stage, it is a state of pure knowledge or Intelligence in which the

---

1. This is a point which should be carefully borne in mind if one is to understand properly the teachings of the Trika and of the Sāṅkhya. When they speak of any one Guṇa being more prominent than the others in a particular manifestation, they do not mean that the others are altogether *absent* from or entirely wanting in that manifestation, but that they are there though only in a comparatively subdued condition. See also below.

feeling is one of bliss no doubt, but without anything of a *moving*, reacting or passional nature in it. Thus the Sattva is—as has been intimated above and as may be now pointed out in passing,—the originator of both *calm* pleasure and enjoyment (rather of a blissful feeling) and also an exalted state of Consciousness in us. Indeed it is the latter which is the real character of an affection by the Sattva, the feeling of bliss being but a concomitant result of it.[1]

Further, as this experience of the Buddhi is one in which there is only the notion of a mere existence—of only the fact that certain things or ideas *are*[2]—without any thought of an 'I' on the part of the Experiencer or any movement of a passion, it is said to be an experience of *Being* only (Sattā-Mātra,): a fact which may account for the name of its chief Affective Feature, namely the Sattva, which literally means Existence, *i. e.* mere being or mere presentation.

So far we have considered Buddhi as the product of only the factors which come into manifestation, in the evolution of the Universe, *prior* to the individual having any experiences of the concrete sense objects. But Buddhi has other contents as well, which are derived from the later experiences of the individual. These are called the Saṁskāras—the refined and, as it were, the distilled essences *abstracted* out of the concrete experiences of one's daily life.[3] These will be considered later. For

---

1. ज्ञानमपि सत्त्वरूपा निर्णयबोधस्य कारणं बुद्धिः । *Tattva-Sandoha* 15.
सुखं सत्त्वं प्रकाशत्वात् प्रकाशो ह्लाद उच्यते । *Tantrāl.*, Āhn. 9.

2. Sattā-mātra.

3. तथाशेषसंस्काराधारत्वात् । *Sānkh. Sū.*, II. 42. See also Vijñāna on it. I have fully explained in *Hindu Realism* how Saṁskāras are produced. See *Hindu Realism*. pp. 103—106.

The Buddhists call Saṁskāras, or, as in Pāli, Saṅkhāras, also by the name of sesa chetasikā which is very significant, as it literally means the last remnants or final results of mental operation.

the present it is enough for our purpose to know (*a*) that 'Buddhi' is what may be spoken of as the memory of the Shuddha-Vidyā Experience produced by the revivification of the dim and indefinite 'Something' of the Prakṛiti to which that experience had been once reduced; (*b*) that it consists of *General* and *Abstract* ideas which as such cannot be pictured by the individual mind of a man in the same way as can a concrete thing, a particular cow for instance, or a concrete act, a particular act of kindness for example; (*c*) that, remaining in the background of or beyond the *personal* consciousness of a man, as Rāma or Jones, it acts as that standard a reference to which is needed before one can *ascertain* the nature of a concrete object of experience as belonging to one 'Species' or another and can form a judgment about it; and (*d*) that, finally, it is an experience of calm joy and pure Consciousness, of mere presentation as such, in which one is quite oblivious of the limited Individual Self as the 'I' of the Experience, and in which there is as yet no moving feeling.

And it is produced from the Prakṛiti, as said above, in much the same way as, and for a similar reason to that which, brings on, in our daily life, a state of wakefulness, following upon a state of deep and profound sleep.

From Buddhi is produced the above mentioned Ahaṅkāra.

Its manifestation from the Buddhi, *i. e.* its *realisation as an Experience after* that of the Buddhi, may again be likened to the stage immediately following that self-oblivious Consciousness which we sometimes have on waking up from a state of sleep, which corresponds in some respects, as we have seen, to the experience of the Buddhi. And it comes to be realised in much the same way and for similar reasons. On waking up—in the sort of case we have taken for our example—first there is the Consciousness of the surroundings, without the thought of the Self as the 'I' of the experience. Then the thought turns to oneself and there is the *conscious* experience, 'I am so and so.'

The manifestation of Ahaṅkāra is not unlike this. It is the realisation of oneself as a particular person—as the 'I am *so and so*'—after the experience of the super-personal Buddhi merely as 'these things or ideas *are*,' without the thought of the 'I' in it.

From this it will be seen that the Ahaṅkāra is not a mere and abstract 'I', but it is always an 'I am *so and so*'. Indeed in our individual experiences as particular persons what constitutes our 'I' has absolutely no other meaning except an 'I am *so and so*'—I am this body, these thoughts, these emotions, here at this place, now at this moment, and so on,—the 'so and so' of the experience being either explicitly formulated in thought or being there implicitly as the basis of the experience, but always *identified* with and as oneself.

In our daily life this 'so and so' consists of the experience we have had from childhood upwards—the 'I' or 'Ego' of every one of us having been *built up* by these. Such an 'I' is, in other words, an *aggregate* of these experiences and of their *concrete* results—the abstract and general results of which are the nature of Buddhi, being beyond the personal Ego,—stored up somewhere in the depth of our being, from where, as has been pointed out above, are contributed those elements in our daily experience which go towards transforming the sense manifold into something more than what is actually 'given' by the senses.

But at the stage we are now considering, the 'so and so' of the Ahaṅkāra cannot be these; for these are had only at a later stage of manifestation. It can, at this stage, consist only of such general elements or aspects of the already experienced Buddhi as are *particularised* for the purpose. And this particularisation takes place in obedience to the same or a similar law which we find in operation in our every day life. It is a process, as will be readily seen, of selecting a *special section* out of a *general whole* and then being 'engaged' on it so as *to make it one's own* either as a particular object of thought or a particular field of operation. It is, in short, a process of *selection* and of making *what is so selected one's own*, as *'my and mine'* or of *building it into one-self* as the 'I',—as for instance, when the body, consisting of materials particularised from a general whole, and built into one's self, is regarded as the 'I' of a man.

Following this process, a special section or aspect of the Buddhi is selected and is regarded by the experiencing entity as *particularly its own* and there arises the experience 'this is mine or these are mine', 'I am this' or 'I am so and so'—there is, in other words, the experience, of what may be called self-apperception.

This realisation of one-self as the 'I' and as the self and owner of a *'particular this,'* as distinguished from the 'All-this', is what is meant by the production of the Ahaṅkāra.

And Ahaṅkāra thus produced consists,—at this stage, let me repeat, and in so far as its elements are personal ones,—of a particularised aspect or aspects of the general Buddhi, and constitutes the 'particular this' or the 'so and so' of the experience. In other words, it is, at this stage, only the notion of a mere *some body*, a limited mere '*I am,*' (asmitā-mātra)[1] both as a 'being' and 'possessor', and not I am '*Rāma*' or '*Jones*' (na tu Chaitro Maitro

---

1. *Yoga Bhāṣhya* ii. 19 with the *Vārttika* on it.

vā ham asmīti). The difference which there is between the Ahaṅkāra thus constituted and the Buddhi consists in the fact that, while the former is the experience "*I am* all this and all this is *mine*", the latter is simply the experience "all this *is*", without as yet the realisation of an 'I' or 'mine' in reference to it.

Further, as Ahaṅkāra exists by making its own certain selected and specialised elements either as a possession or as itself, it is essentially a thing of which the function is what may be called 'appropriation' or 'self-arrogation' or identification—in Sanskrit, Abhimāna—by engaging itself in, or intently fixing the thought on, what is so selected (Abhi, on, about and Man, to think or feel). Indeed, Ahaṅkāra may be said to be only this *power* or *energy* of 'self-arrogation'—of building up materials into an 'Ego'; and, being a power, it is a product, ultimately, of Shakti through the intermediate Prakṛiti which obviously is a mode of the Divine Energy.[1]

Finally, Ahaṅkāra is what may be called a *static* condition, to a certain extent at least, of the individual existence, inasmuch as there is as yet *very* little movement in it. It is the State or Experience of Self-realisation as the personal Ego, just preceding the state of movement, in much the same way as the state of Self-recollection, following the Self-oblivious consciousness of the first waking up from sleep of our illustration, is a state of *comparative* motionlessness preceding movements which

---

1. It is this Ahaṅkāra which, according to the teaching of the Buddha also (as represented in the Pāli Piṭakas), holds together the ingredients of Nāma-Rūpa making up an individual being. See, for instance, the story of the Bhikṣhu Upasena, as given in the *Saṁyutta Nikāya* (xxxv. 69, Pāli Text Soc. edition) wherein we are told how Upasena's body was scattered because there was no Ahaṅkāra up-holding it.

are to follow directly. It is a state of experience of what may be called a mental stock-taking on the part of the now limited experiencer, viewing round and realising, as it were, what he *is* and what he can do; and as such it may be said to correspond to the Sadā-shiva state of the Pure Way, mentioned before.[1] It is a state of forming *resolves* as to what to do, by a survey and realisation of what one is and is capable of doing—by feeling oneself as a *somebody* with a *will* to do. It is thus a state in which, as in the Sadā-Shiva-Tattva, the *will* aspect of the Divine Shakti is most manifest. But it is also a state in which, as said above, the Experiencer *identifies* himself with the 'so and so' of the experience. And as this identification means—unlike the Sadā-shiva state where there is as yet no *all* this or some this—*some movement* of thought and feeling, as it were, *towards* and all round the 'so and so', it is a state in which there is already manifest, to some extent at least, also that Affective Feature of the Prakṛiti which *can* affect the experiencer as such a *moving feeling, i. e.* the Rajas Guṇa which was more or less suppressed in the previous Buddhic State. That is to say, Ahaṅkāra is an experience in which the will aspect of the Divine Shakti and the Rajas Guṇa of the Prakṛiti are the more dominant elements.[2]

But, although Ahaṅkāra is an experience in which the Rajas is in more prominent manifestation, it contains

---

1. Ante p. 74.

2. इच्छास्य रजोरूपाहंकृतिरासीदहंप्रतीतिकरी। *Tattva*-*Sandoha*, 14.

Rajas is that Affective Feature of the Prakṛiti which affects *primarily* as a *moving feeling*, or as some form of activity. Its affection is 'painful' only in a secondary sense, just as the blissful effect of Sattva, which affects *primarily* as Prakāsha—'revelation' or 'light', *i. e.* mere presentation—is only secondary. Compare—

दुःखं रजः क्रियात्मत्वात् क्रिया हि तदतत्क्रमः। *Tantrāl.*, Ahn. 9.

in it the other two Guṇas as well, only in a subdued and suppressed form, in the same way as there are the Tamas and Rajas in the Buddhi, even though Sattva may be most prominently manifest in it. Indeed Prakṛiti, being but the Guṇas in a state of equipoise, all its derivatives, such as the Buddhi, Ahaṅkāra and the others to be mentioned later, cannot but have in them all the three Guṇas, even though it is only one of them which is prominently manifest at a time while the remaining two subsist in a subdued form. This is a point which should never be lost sight of, if one is to understand the Trika, or the Sāṅkhya, doctrines in regard to these later phases of manifestation.

From Ahaṅkāra again is produced the above mentioned Manas.

From what has been already said about Manas, it will be seen that it is a state of activity—it being busily engaged in building up images, as fast as the senses supply the manifold of the external universe. But this is not its only function. It has many activities besides. For it is also that something in us which constantly *moves* from sense to sense, as what is called attention, and co-operates with the senses before the latter can 'give' us anything at all. There may be the whole world before us and the senses in contact with and acted on by the different stimulating features of that world, yet they may not produce any 'sensation' whatever, if what is ordinarily called 'mind' is absent from them—if one is, as it is put *'absent-minded.'* The senses, therefore, must receive the co-operation of this something vaguely called mind before they can at all act. Nor can this 'mind' be any other than what builds up images out of the 'given' of the sense; that is to say, it is none other than the Manas; because Manas is the factor which comes into operation *immediately* after the manifold of sense is given, all other elements necessary for the perception of a 'thing' as a cow or a horse, being supplied *afterwards*. *First* the picture is built and *then* it is substantiated with and assimilated to the other necessary materials of previous personal experiences held together in and as the personal 'I' or Ahaṅkāra, and compared with the general ideas of the Buddhi—and indeed gone through several other operations in the other and deeper factors of our nature as will be seen later. And if any 'instrument' has to co-operate with the senses before they can at all give us anything, it must be this picture-making instrument, that is to say, the Manas; because Manas as it were lies next to the senses and *intervenes*, so to say, between the senses on the one hand and the Ahaṅkāra on the other, with the Buddhi lying beyond it still, as can be inferred from the successive operations of these. Nor need we suppose that the *something* which obviously does and must co-operate with the senses and which is referred to vaguely as 'mind' or 'attention', is other than the image-making and concreting Manas, lying, as it were, between this latter on the one hand and the senses on the other. There is no ground for such a supposition. For not only are we never conscious of the existence of such a thing, but it is far simpler and far more natural to suppose that what co-operates on the one hand severally with the senses,—thus receiving from them all the manifold elements they can supply—and, on the other, gathers them together and builds them up into the concrete images of perception, should be one and the same thing.

Manas is, in this sense also,[1] a concreting and synthesising factor. Not only does it put together the 'manifold' supplied by a single sense as so many points or 'pin-pricks' and build them up into an image, but it also 'puts together' and concretes the various sets of maifolds supplied by the different senses and makes of hem a single concrete image.

1 See *ante* p. 95.

Thus it is, that Manas is intensely active and restless[1] as it moves constantly, on the one hand from sense to sense, and on the other from the senses to the Ahaṅkāra to which it 'hands over' the sense-manifold after it has been transformed into images to be presently endowed with other elements by the Ahaṅkāra itself from its own store-house.

Manas is, in other words, a state of activity—a *Kinetic State*—following that of the comparatively Static Ahaṅkāra.

And it follows the Ahaṅkāra in much the same way—and for more or less the same reasons—as the state of Self-recollection, *i. e*, the second state on waking from sleep in our example, is followed by that of activity when a man begins to move or move about.

The mutual relation of the three States of Buddhi, Ahaṅkāra and Manas may not inaptly be illustrated, at least in certain of their aspects, by the behaviour of a cat or a tiger when catching prey.

Let us suppose that our tiger was sleeping. Then suddenly he is waked up by the movements of some animal he can devour; and he is all awake, only eyeing his prey and *without any thought of himself*. This may be likened to Buddhi.

Then he makes a *resolve* to kill the animal and gathers *himself* up and assumes a crouching position—a motionless state of *Self-possession*, but one which is going immediately to be followed by one of activity. This is not unlike Ahaṅkāra.

The next moment, he takes a tremendous leap and is immediately on his prey, and there is a great struggle

---

1. See below, p. 117. notes; 1,2 also compare:

चञ्चलं हि मनः कृष्ण प्रमाथि बलवद् दृढम् ।

Bhag. Gitā, vi. 34

and fierce activity. This is not quite a bad picture of the Manas.

This illustration would be still more complete if we could suppose that our tiger remained simultaneously in the three positions—existing simultaneously as three tigers, the last as the outcome of the second and this of the first. For, we must not forget that when Manas is produced from Ahaṅkāra and the latter from Buddhi, neither this nor the Ahaṅkāra ceases to exist, but on the contrary they remain what they have always been, even after their respective products have come into existence.

But although so active, Manas is not an experience in which the Rajas,—the Affective Feature of the Prakṛiti, affecting primarily as a moving feeling (moving the experiencer into activity of some sort)—is most manifest. For the activities of Manas by *themselves* produce neither any *intelligent* and *illuminating* results, nor any *moving* feeling of pleasure and pain. The images which the Manas builds up by its activity are by themselves never of an illuminating nature; *i. e.* they do not and cannot reveal themselves independently to the experiencer. Before they can be so revealed and realised as objects of perception, they will have to be taken up, as we have seen, not only to the Ahaṅkāra but also to the Buddhi without whose intelligent light they would be but dark forms, unseen and unknown by the Experiencer, and the efforts of the Manas but blind and 'stupid' gropings in the dark.[1] Nor can the images built up by the Manas affect, of themselves, the experiencer so as to *move* him in any way until and unless the experiencer identifies himself with them by

1. Compare the famous saying of Kant that perceptions (anschauung) without conceptions are *blind.*

Ahaṅkāra, *i. e.* by making them his own in feeling and experience. The Manas by itself, being thus an experience of activity in the dark, unseen and unrevealed by the light of Buddhi, and not moving the experiencer till he identifies himself with it in feeling, is one in which the Tamas Guṇa is the most manifest.[1]

But, although blind and moving and working in the dark, still Manas is an experience of groping, of *seeking*, however unintelligently. It is therefore the seat of 'desires'. Indeed Manas is 'desire' incarnate.[2]

And, as said above, this manas comes into manifestation from the Ahaṅkāra.

The Means and General Principles of Sensible Experience: The Five Senses, Five Powers of Action, and Five General Objects of Perception

But Manas is not the only product of Ahaṅkāra. Two other classes or groups of factors are also produced from it, *viz*:—

a. The decad of Indriyas or powers, mentioned above. (pp. 48–49), consisting of the quintad of the Powers or capacities of sense perception and the quintad of the powers of action;[3] and

---

1. तस्य क्रिया तमोमयमूर्त्तिर्मन उच्यते विकल्पकरी । *Tattva Sandoha.* 15.

Tamas is the Feature which affects as the *want* of Prakāsha, or of light of consciousness, as the Sattva does as Prakāsha. Compare—

मोहस्तमो वरणकः प्रकाशाभावयोगतः । *Tantrāl.* Ahn. 9.

2. यदा प्रार्थयते किंचित् तदा भवति सा मनः । *Mahābhār*..........

3. According to the Buddha also the Indriyas are the outcome of Ahaṅkāra. Comp. अस्मीति खो पन भिक्खवे अधिगते अथ पञ्चन्नम् इन्द्रियानम् अवक्कन्ति होति । *Saṁyutta Nik.* XXII. 47. 5., P. T. S. Edn.

b. The quintad of general objects of the special senses (also mentioned above pp. 48–49) or the primary elements of the sense-manifold, *i. e.*, the Tanmātras, as they are technically called in Sanskrit.

Before considering how these are produced from the Ahaṅkāra, let us clearly understand what the first group, *i. e.* the Indriyas, really are.[1]

By Indriyas, the Shaiva Philosopher means not merely the physical organs of hearing, feeling-by-touch, seeing, tasting and smelling, and the so-called muscular sense and the bodily organs of action, but also those powers or faculties of the Purusha—rather the Purusha as endowed with and manifesting these faculties and powers —which show themselves as operating through or by these physical organs. While they may therefore be spoken of as 'senses' and organs, we must, in speaking of them thus, bear this distinction carefully in mind.

The Indriyas are divided primarily into two classes which may be spoken of, *in reference only to their physical manifestations but not as they are in themselves*, as the sensory and motor nervous systems—in Sanskrit, the Buddhīndriyas or Jñānendriyas, the powers of mere *perception* or the senses; and Karmendriyas, the powers of action.

The former, *i. e.* the Jñānendriyas or senses proper, are five, namely:

the Power of hearing

do of feeling-by-touch (in which both the temperature and the contact or tactile senses are included. For reasons for this, as well as for the

1. For references to the original texts on the whole of this section on the Indriyas or Powers see Appendix VIII.

real notion of the Hindu philosophers, who knew this distinction well, in regard to these two senses now recognised by Western psychologists as quite distinct from one another, see Appendix IX).

the Power of seeing
do of tasting
and do of smelling

The Karmendriyas or Powers of action are also five, namely :

The Power of expression such as speaking
do of grasping or handling
do of locomotion
do of excretion (voiding, spitting, expectorating &c.)
do of sexual action, (comprising all sexual activity, *i. e.* all activity which a person of one sex is moved to, or does, perform towards another person of the opposite sex, and which, when so performed, results in overwhelming *restfulness* and of which the real *motive, i. e.* moving Force or power, is this desire for this particular kind of restfulness.)

In the physical body these five Powers of action *happen* (of course for adequate reasons which need not, however, be entered into here) to be represented respectively by the vocal organ, hands, feet, anus (for voiding only) and the sex organ; but it should be clearly borne in mind that these are *not* the five powers of action themselves. These physical limbs and organs are no doubt ordinarily the means whereby the operation of the active powers are carried on. Indeed, they have been evolved for the purpose by the Purușha *desiring* to act in these five ways. But if any of these may happen to be disabled, the power of action, for which it served as an outward means, may still find some other way of accomplishing its task. If, for instance, the feet are disabled, as they may in the case of a cripple, the power of locomotion, which is a superphysical power, may find an outward means in the hands with the help of which a man may be moving about—not so efficiently certainly as with the feet, which have been evolved specially for the purpose through ages of practice, still effectively enough within limits.

Similarly, while the five physical organs of the ear, skin, eye, nose and palate represent, and serve as the outward means of operation for, the five senses of perception, the latter are not only not identical with them but are not even absolutely dependent on them. In India it has been always recognized that there are certain ways, known to the Yogins, whereby they can accomplish all that can be done by means of these physical organs without the use of the latter. In the West too, it is not unknown to hypnotists that the hypnotised subject can perceive things—specially can smell and taste—even when no use of the special physical organs ordinarily necessary for the purpose is made.

Now these Powers of the Spirit—five powers of perception differentiated from a general power of mere awareness (*i. e.* vidyā, see Appendix IX) and five of action, *i. e.* the ten Indriyas—come into manifestation, as said above, from the Ahaṅkāra and they do so simultaneously with the Manas. The way they are produced is as follows :—

We have seen that the Manas is the seat of desires, or rather Manas is the Purușha when it has reached that state of manifestation in which it is endowed with or has developed desires. Now these desires are always either to perceive in one or other of the five ways of perception; *viz*:

to hear,
to feel-by-touch (heat or cold, smoothness or roughness and so on),
to see,
to taste,
and to smell;

or, to act in one or other of the five ways of action *viz:*

to express (to speak)
to handle (to grasp or hold)
to move about
to excrete (to void, expectorate and so on)
and to act being prompted by a sensual impulse with a view to and to remain *still* when so enjoining what is 'loved' and is felt as one's own self. (svarūpa-vishrānti)

In other words *desire*, as represented by Manas, can never exist by itself. It is desire either to *perceive* or to *act*. And therefore the moment there arises such a desire in the Purușha when it has reached the Ahaṅkāra Stage, and therewith Manas is produced, that very moment the powers, *i. e.* the Indriyas, to perceive or to act are also evolved. And as the desire, *i. e.* Manas, arises, and can arise, only in these ten forms—five for perception and five for action— the ten Indriyas are also produced, simultaneously with the Manas as Desire, in their tenfold forms.

Not only this. The moment the five Indriyas of perception are produced, what are called the five Tanmātras, that is to say, the five primary elements of perception mentioned above, also come into manifestation from the same Ahaṅkāra.[1] Because the Indriyas can have really no meaning, and really no existence, whatever without the objects with which they are inseparably correlated. The Indriya of hearing has, for instance, no meaning without something to hear,—that is, some sound. Similarly, the Indriya of feeling-by-touch, seeing, tasting and smelling have no meaning without a simultaneous reference to *some thing* to feel-by-touch, something to see, taste and smell. Therefore the moment the Manas arises as desire, the Ahaṅkāra takes a triple form, as for instance,

I desire[1] to-see[2] some-colour[3].

In this experience the 'I' is the Ahankāra in the background; and the three forms of its manifestation are the 'Desire' which is Manas, the Seeing which is the Indriya, (in this case of vision) and the Notion of some colour which is the object of perception. That the Manas as desire and the sense of sight as a power of thePuruṣha are the modifications of the Ahaṅkāra will be readily seen. The object also—the notion of some colour—can be nothing else but only a form of the Ahaṅkāra realised as a thing *projected outside*, as there is no other source from which it can come to the Ahaṅkāra, and as it is its *own* perception: for anything that is any body's *own* is really a part of his own Self as a person, *i. e.* of his Ahaṅkāra. In later experience such a thing can, *in a certain sense*, be 'given' from outside first and then woven into the Ahaṅkāra and made its own. But at the stage we are now considering there is no such experience possible; and therefore this 'perception' which is the 'own' thing on the part of a particular Ahaṅkāra can be evolved only from itself.

---

1. For references to texts on the Tanmātras, see Appendix X.

Thus it happens that with the manifestation of the five Indriyas of perception there are also evolved, from the Ahaṅkāra, the corresponding objects of perception.

But these objects at this stage can be, every one of them, only of a most general character, that is to say, they can be only the general mental conceptions of

Sound-as-such, as distinguished from particular forms of sound *i. e.* sounds of various pitch, tone and so on;

Feel-as-such, as distinguished from the varying forms of it, experienced as cold, warmth and heat, hardness, softness and the like;

Colour-as-such, as distinguished from particular forms, varieties of shades of colour,—red, green, blue and so on;

Flavour-as-such, as distinguished from particular forms of flavour,—sweet, bitter, sour and so on; and

Odour-as-such, as distinguished from particular forms of odour—fragrant, foul and so on;

because, in the first place, there is as yet no reason why there should be a perception, even a mental perception, of any one particular form or shade, rather than another, of any of these sense objects. Such particulars are perceived only when, at a later stage with the experience of a physical world, we have these particulars as the 'given' of the experience, so far as these are supplied by these purely special senses of hearing, feeling-by-touch, seeing, tasting and smelling. And the very fact that we can ever form the general ideas of these sense-objects, *i. e.* of sound, temperature, colour, flavour and odour as such, as distinguished from the particulars of these, shows that these must already exist somewhere in some part or aspect of our nature as facts of experience; and remaining there serve as a standard, reference to which alone can enable us to talk of the particulars in purely general terms[1]. If the *general notions* of the particulars of each sense object were not present in our minds, there would be no chance of our forming these from the particulars 'given' by the senses as the physical facts of experience—the particulars being all that we thus get—for that would really mean the very impossible task of building up something which we have never known, the creation of a thing which is totally different in *kind* from what we have already experienced in some shape or other either in parts or as a whole. And surely we never experience in the physical world, by means of the senses as represented in the body, any such thing as colour in general or colour-as-such, sound-as-such, and so on. These, therefore, must already be experienced in some other state, before the particulars of physical experience can ever be referred to in general terms.

And they are experienced at the stage we are now considering, when they are produced from the Ahaṅkāra, as mere general notions of *somethings* heard, seen and so on, because—and this is the second reason—these general notions of the particulars of the special senses only cannot belong to the generals of the Buddhi, which contains the general ideas not only of these special sense particulars but of *all* things particular. The general of a special sense is no doubt *general* in regard to the particulars of that sense only; but it is itself only a particular in regard to what constitutes the contents of the Buddhi—it being but a *particular* aspect or facet out of a number of aspects which make up a thing, as the latter must necessarily have other aspects as well. The general notion of the 'cow', that is, cow as a species, is not merely the notion of colour-as-such or sound-as-such but

---

1 For a consideration, from the Hindu point of view, of this doctrine of the previous existence or pre-suppositions of these 'generals' see Appendix VII.

a something which possesses both colour-as-such, and sound-as-such, besides many other attributes all no doubt of a general character; for a particular cow is a thing which has particular colours, sound of a particular sort and also other attributes of which each is only a particular form of a general type. The notion of the cow, therefore, as a species, is a general notion in which the generals of colours, sounds and the rest are still further generalised into what has these even as so many particulars.

Thus the general of the particulars of a special sense is only a particular in regard to the general of the Buddhi and is thus different from the latter.

And it is only these generals of the sense-particulars which come into manifestation when the pure 'I am' of the Ahaṅkāra experiences itself as a being desiring to hear, to feel-by-touch, to see, taste or smell something, as they alone can be the objects of the perception now desired, they being specialised from the generals of the Buddhi by means of, or through, the intermediate experience of self-realisation, as 'I', that is, as the Ahaṅkāra.

And they come into manifestation simultaneously with the Buddhindriyas as the inevitable second term of the indissoluble relation which subsists between the senses and their objects.

These general notions of the particulars, which latter alone are 'given' by the five special senses as represented in the body, are called the *Tanmātras* *i. e.* the general elements of the particulars of sense perception; (lit. That only). These Tanmātras, therefore, are, as said above, the following:

1. Sound-as-such (Shabda-Tanmātra),
2. Feel-as-such (Sparsha-Tanmātra),
3. Colour-as-such (Rūpa-Tanmātra),
4. Flavôur-as-such (Rasa-Tanmātra),

and 5. Odour-as-such (Gandha-Tanmātra).

And as they thus come into manifestation, there are also produced at the same time—from the same Ahaṅkāra, but as the results of the *reaction* of these—the Karmendriyas mentioned above. How they are thus produced may be shown as follows :—

There is a tendency in us that, when we hear some one speak, we often want to respond and speak back. This instinct is seen very strongly preserved in certain lower animals: in jackals, for instance, so that when a jackal hears another cry out, he also instinctively responds and howls back. There are some birds also which possess this instinct in a marked degree; so much so that fowlers in certain parts of India take advantage of it, and find out the whereabouts of such birds by either making a tamed bird of the species utter a cry or by cleverly imitating themselves the cry of the bird. The moment this is done, all birds of the species in the neighbourhood begin to respond at once and the fowlers spot them exactly.[1]

Following this tendency, when, with the evolution of the power of hearing, sound-as-such is realised, there is also the realisation, on the part of the spirit (as it now at this stage is *i. e.* the Puruṣha with these powers only but still without a body) of the power to respond ;—it desires to respond *i. e.* to speak out in response to the sound heard, and therewith the *power to respond* that is to express (the Vāg-indriya) is evolved.

Then, we find that if anything tickles us or we feel too hot or too cold in any *part* of the body we instinctively put our hand to that part—there is an instinctive

---

1 I have known a clever ventriloquist to make wild Indian cuckoos (kokila) respond in this fashion.

desire to *handle* that part, rather, to handle what so tickles us or makes us feel thus hot or cold.

Following this instinct, when the Sparsha-tanmātra is realised, *i. e.* the sensation of Feel-as-such is produced, there arises also the desire to handle what so produced the sensation and therewith the *power to handle, i. e.*, the Hastendriya comes into existence.

Similarly, when we see a thing suddenly bursting into view, there is an instinctive tendency in us to move or run away from, or, as in some cases, towards, it. No doubt it is now greatly checked in us by ages of training and education. But it can be seen strongly present in lower animals. And following this instinct, when, with the evolution of the power of Vision (or Darshanendriya), the colour-as-such or Rūpa-Tanmātra is realised, the *power to move away from* or *towards* it, *i. e.*, the *power of locomotion*, the Pādendriya, is developed.

Again, when a thing is suddenly put into our mouth the first and instinctive tendency is, not to see how we may like its taste, but to *throw* it out or eject it. A similar *tendency* gives rise to the *power to discard* from our system, which at the stage we are considering is still without a physical body, the moment the sensation of Flavour-as-such is experienced with the evolution of the sense of taste.

Finally, the experience of Odour-as-such gives rise to what is activity really in a negative sense. For it is an *act* of enjoyment and therefore restfulness, and no *movement* such as activity generally implies. And it comes about in much the same way as when, with all the other senses closed and inactive (as the situation at the super-physical stage of manifestation we are considering must be regarded to be) we are made to smell some odour which is more or less of an indifferent character and to which odour-as-such may, to a certain extent, be compared. Such an experience leads neither to an activity of responding as when hearing a sound, nor of handling, locomotion, nor throwing out and rejecting. If anything, it puts one *to rest* and sleep in a state of *passive* enjoyment.

Thus corresponding with the five special senses or Jñānendriyas and as their *reactions* on the Puruṣha there are produced the five powers or capacities to act, *i. e.*, the five Karmendriyas, which are:

1. The power to respond by making sounds or speaking—the Vāgindriya
2. The power of handling—the Hastendriya
3. The power of moving away from and towards, *i. e.*, of locomotion—the pādendriya
4. The power of discarding or throwing out—the pāyvindriya

and 5. The power of being *passively restful* and enjoying something by which one is at the same time overcome and prevented from moving, and being united with which one feels as though one has realised one's self—one's very heart's desire and does not want to move out, as when uniting sexually, *i. e.* embracing or otherwise;—the Upasthendriya.

From Ahaṅkāra, then, there really evolves a threefold production, *viz:*

1. Manas and the Jñānendriyas. (Mind and senses)
2. The Karmendriyas (Powers of action)

and 3. The general objects of the Jñānendriyas *i. e.* the Tanmātras.

They are however not to be regarded as things existing independently by themselves, but as the endowments of the Purusha which, at this stage, is Ahaṅkāra together with, or enveloped in, these, as well as the Ahaṅkāra in itself as such, the Buddhi behind it and all the rest, standing, as it were in the far back-ground. The individual as thus endowed may be termed the 'Soul'.

The Principles of Materiality: The Five Bhutas

This stage reached, the Purusha or as we may now call it, the Soul, is nearly ready for its round of existence and experiences as a full fledged individual. There remains but one more step to take to accomplish this fully. This last step may be spoken of as the *Materialisation* of the Soul *i. e.* of the Purusha with its endowments.

And it happens in the following way:—[1]

In the last stage the objects of experience were, as we have seen, of a general character—sound-, feel-, colour-, flavour- and odour-as-such without the perception of any variations in any of them. But however much these may be perceived as objects of the senses in the beginning, *i. e.*, when they are first produced, they gradually cease to be the objects of such perception in obedience to the same principle which makes the Experiencer lose sight of the 'All-this' of the Shuddha-Vidyā state, or of the Generals of the Buddhi at a later stage of manifestation: the same principle which we find in operation also in daily life, ultimately due to Māyā, the 'Self-hiding' aspect of the Divine Shakti. We find in our daily experience that if we are face to face with a merely homogenous something without any variation in it, we gradually lose sight of it as such a thing—unless we are endowed with, or have already developed in us, that

1 For the original texts bearing on this section see Appendix XI

Vidyā Shakti[1] of the Yogin which, being the opposite of Māyā, can remain fully alive to it and can keep holding it before him as a vivid and clear object of experience. We find that when placed in such a situation, our minds eagerly seek a change in it—a variation or variations in the object of experience—or we fall asleep, which however leads to the same result, inasmuch as sleep itself means a change in the experience to be followed by a still further one when we wake up. Following this principle then, when the Soul is face to face with the mere sound-as-such for a time, it ceases to notice it at all, however much the Soul may have been affected thereby when it first arose as an object of experience, in exactly the same way as sound would cease to be perceived consciously if any of us now found himself drowned in an absolutely homogeneous sea of sound from all directions without any variation whatsoever. Such a volume of sound would certainly be perceived as such by him when it first burst out; but after a while his ears would get accustomed to it and he would either not notice it—it growing into a normal sorrounding—or he would fall asleep, only to wake up to perceive a change. Or, it may happen—as it certainly does and must happen at the stage of evolution we are considering, there being at that stage no reason why the soul should fall asleep—that the Soul already having an experience of sound and now not noticing it any longer, eagerly seeks to hear it again. But it can do so only by *conceiving* variations in it: such a conception on its part of a *variation* or *variations* being possible because there is contained in the general conception all the elements of the particulars, in much the same way as the Colour rays are already contained in the white light of the Sun; or, for the matter of that, the whole of the Universal Variety is contained in the single experience of Parama Shiva.

---

1 Vidyā Shakti enables one to overcome the effect of Māyā, acting in opposition to Māyā; see *Īsh. Prat.*, III. i. 7.

Thus it is that from the general perception of the sound-as-such there arises the perception of the sound-particulars.

Similarly from the perception of Feel-, Colour-, Flavour- and Odour-as-such there also arise the perceptions of the several particulars or varieties of these.

Not only this. Along with the manifestation of varieties in the generals of these sense-objects, there are also produced some very important results. What these are and how they are produced would be best understood if we could, in imagination, put ourselves now in a position which would be similar to what must have been the situation when these varieties were first experienced by a Soul.

Let us imagine ourselves to be present face to face with, indeed to be drowned in, a sea of homogeneous sound which has already become, in the way described above, no sound at all, that is, has ceased to form an object of perception; and let us also imagine that there are no other objects whatsoever, as would be the case under the circumstances we are trying to picture, the other generals of Feel, Colour, Flavour and Odour having equally and for equal reasons ceased to be perceived. Then let us further imagine that there suddenly arises, or, which is the same thing, is perceived a variety of sounds. What would be the experience that would instantly, instinctively and *necessarily* accompany or rather follow, this perception of a variety of sounds, as it were, *all over the Soul*, as it would now be, there being as yet no *localised* sense of hearing as there is as yet no physical body. It goes almost without saying that it would be the experience of a *something* that goes in *all Directions* (dishaḥ); that is to say of Wide Expanse or Empty-Space (Avakāsha in Sanskrit, as distinguished from *filled* Space which gives rise to the experience of relativity of Positions or positional relations, (Desha in

Sanskrit). For, the moment such sounds are perceived that very moment, it will also be realised that they are proceeding from *all directions*, corresponding to the perception which will be experienced, for reasons stated above, *all over the Soul* [1].

---

1. Ākāsha or Ether is nothing but the Dishaḥ or '*Directions*' *i. e. lines* of what may be called *forces* spreading out or radiating everywhere. These *lines, directions* or Dishaḥ are symbolised as the 'hairs' of Shiva who is therefore called Vyomakeshā, *i. e.*, 'He who has for his hairs the Vyoman which is another name for both Dish or Direction and Akāsha or Space (See Nirukta, I. 3 and 6). The word Vyoman is derived from the root 'Ve' or 'Vā' meaning 'weaving' as with threads, together with the prefix ' Vi ' meaning diversity. From this derivation of the term, it will be readily seen how ' Space ' is most appropriately called Vyoman. For Space is essentially made up of these Dishaḥ or directions, going everywhere as lines of force, which uphold all things in the Universe in various positional relations (see *Hindu Realism*, pp. 54–61). These lines interweave themselves into that universally enveloping fabric which is Space. (The simile of all Space, and indeed the whole universe, being thus ' woven ' like a cloth is met with several times in the Veda).

That Dishaḥ or ' Directions ' as the essence of all Space is inseparably connected with ' Hearing,' which again has no meaning without reference to Sound, is an idea which also we find repeatedly mentioned in the Upaniṣhads.

That the all-upholding Dishaḥ, as the 'hairs of Shiva,' spreading everywhere, are *Lines of Force* need not be an absurd idea. The existence of similar *lines* would seem to be recognised even by modern Western Science, in certain respects at any rate. We are told how there are what would appear as 'lines' of Force radiating from the poles of a 'magnet', which 'lines' being cut by a conductor give rise to an electrical current. Electricity is again, we are told, somehow mysteriously connected with Ether, which would seem to be the same thing as the Ākāsha of the Hindus, that is, Ākāsha which is made up essentially of the lines of the Dishaḥ or of the 'Hairs

That is to say from the experience of variety in the uniformity of Sound-as-such, there would result also the experience of a Wide Expanse or Space. This Wide Expanse, that is this *Something* spreading in *all directions*, however, is the same as 'Nothing.' This 'something' going out in all directions, therefore being *practically* 'Nothing', the experience of it also results, in practice, in one of Vacuity or Empty-Space as said above. In Sanskrit it is called Ākāsha, by which is meant both a *something* which goes out in *all directions* and makes all Space or *locale* possible; and also Vacuity or Empty-Space. It may perhaps be translated by Ether, (rather, Etheriality), as this is also conceived as existing and spreading in *all directions*, taking note however of the fact that while what is spoken of as 'Ether' is regarded in the West as having movements—even though they may be merely vibratory movements—and as the medium for the transmission of light, Ākāsha as conceived in Hindu Philosophy (at least of some schools)[1] has no movements

---

of Shiva'. May not these 'lines' of the magnetic field be connected with the *lines* of Dishaḥ as the lines of Etherial Energy ?

That such a connection may not be impossible will be apparent from the fact that the Earth is regarded as a vast electrical reservoir—the 'common reservoir' as it is called. It is also regarded as a vast magnet from which magnetic lines of Force are constantly emanating. In the same way, the centre of the universe may be conceived as a still vaster magnet or electrical reservoir, from which similar lines of Force are undoubtedly emanating in all directions. And what can this centre of the Universe be but the Divine Reality, which again is the innermost Self of every being ? The lines of Force emanating from this centre would then be the Dishaḥ of the Hindus, the 'Hairs' of their Shiva, to which must be essentially related the lines of Force which demonstrably emanate from every magnet.

1. See *Hindu Realism*, p. 52

whatever, nor has it any such function. Inasmuch as this Ākāsha, Ether or Etherial factor, though very real, *i. e.* as real, say, as the solidity of the earth, is for all practical purposes and as realised in experience (not merely inferred from *other* facts of experience) a mere 'Nothing' or Vacuity, we may also call it the Principle of Vacuity.

It is this realisation of the Ākāsha or Ether *i. e.* this experiencing the Principle of Vacuity, in the way mentioned above, which is described in the technical language of the system, when it is said that

> "From variety produced in the Tanmātra of Sound there is produced *Ākāsha,*"

And this is said, because there need be no other experience whatsoever for the realisation of these varieties of Sound but that of '*all directions*', of Wide Expanse, or, what is the same thing, of an *indefinite something* going out in *all directions.* There may be other experiences, as indeed, there will be at a later stage; but these need not *necessarily* be there or *necessarily* precede that of *Ākāsha.*

Further, the experience of Ākāsha is a necessary one, following inevitably and necessarily, as we have seen, from that of the varieties of Sound.

Next let us suppose that we are drowned in a sea of uniform temperature *i. e.*, the simplest and lightest form of Feel which has already ceased to be perceived as an object, and that there are as yet no other objects but the already produced varieties of Sound—as would be the case under the circumstances we are considering. Then, let us further suppose that there arises a variety in this uniform and homogeneous temperature and we begin to feel more hot or more cold, a freezing or burning sensation. What would be the necessarily and inevitably consequent experience and how should we feel these varieties in temperature most? It would be, as but a little reflection will show, the experience of movements like that of air or the aerial atmosphere; that is, of what may be called aeriality—technically Vāyu (lit. the air). There need not necessarily be any other experience whatsover for the realisation of variations in temperature but that of aeriality or movements, like the air-currents, although there *may* be, as later on there *will be*, other experiences as well, accompanying that of variations in temperature. And being a necessary accompaniment of this nature, the experience of aeriality is said to be produced from the experience of variations in that of Feel-as-such.

Or, speaking technically, from the Variations produced in the Sparsha-Tanmātra, there comes into manifestation, Vāyu *i. e.* Aeriality.

Let us again suppose we are face to face with an all-enveloping mass of Colour-as-such which, for reasons mentioned above, has already ceased to form an object of experience, although there may be present in the experience at this stage, the already produced perceptions of the variations of Sound and Feel and of Ākāsha and Vāyu. Then, let us imagine there suddenly arises the experience of a variety of Colours. What would be the necessarily consequent experience when this is realised? The obvious answer would perhaps be that it is the experience of Form and Shape (Rūpa) without which no shade of Colour is ever perceived. But a little reflection will show that it would really be the experience of a *something*, some power or energy, which *builds up, transforms or destroys* such forms. For, when there suddenly arises a patch of Colour in the vacancy of the horizon, it no doubt is seen as a shape or form of some sort. But this 'form' may be said to be the same thing as the Colour, because without it colour, as thus perceived at the time, has hardly any meaning. And therefore the perception of colours of this type means really the same thing as the perception of forms; so much so that, instead of saying that there arose the experience of a variety of Colours one might as well say there arose the experience of a variety of forms.[1] The experience of form, therefore, cannot be called a *consequent* experience in the same way as Ākāsha is the consequent experience of a variety of Sounds, or Aeriality is that of the variation in Feel. It is rather an *identical* experience—the experience of a particular colour being the *same* as that of a particular form. The experience which is really a consequent one in this case, is that of a something, *some power* or *energy* which *produces, transforms,* or *destroys* these forms: for, as the colour-forms are experienced in succession, they are perceived as coming into existence, changing and disappearing, giving rise to the experience of a something which so produces, changes or destroys them—burns them into, or out of, a shape or shapes. This *burning something,* burning and flaring up into various shapes and forms or burning them out, is technically called Agni in Sanskrit (lit. Fire), by which term, however, we must not understand anything—and it cannot be too strongly emphasised, in view of the numerous and gross misconceptions that have been formed of its meaning—but this energy or power of which the only function is combustion or chemical action (Jvalana or Pāka) which again means simply building, producing or reproducing and destroying shapes, bringing shapes and forms into existence from what is formless, and changing one form into some other or many others and *vice-versa.*

Thus it is, that from the experience of variety in

1. The Sanskrit word Rūpa means both colour and form.

Colour-as-such, there arises the experience of the *form-builder* (the formative agency or simply Formativity). Or speaking technically, from variety produced in the Rūpa-tanmātra, there comes into manifestation Agni, the form-building, (and therefore the form-destroying) Principle, or Formativity.

Next, let us imagine that our experience of Flavour-as-such, which has already ceased to be an object of perception, changes into that of a variety of Flavours. The necessarily consequent experience to this would be, as can be easily seen, that of 'moisture', *i. e.*, liquidity; for what is tasted, *i. e.*, different flavours, is always found accompanied with the feeling of moisture without there *necessarily* being any other sensation accompanying it.

This need not be regarded as a strange idea on account of the fact that, unlike the senses of sight, hearing and feeling-by-touch, the sense of tasting plays such a small and unimportant part, and that it seems simply absurd to assert that, from this comparatively unimportant experience of tasting a variety of flavours, there is produced so vast a result as the experience of liquidity, which forms so great a portion of the physical world.

For, we must not forget, that at the stage we are considering, there is as yet no physical body of the soul and the senses are therefore not localised as they are in the body. The sense of taste as well as that of smell, are, therefore, like all other senses, as it were all over the Soul, instead of being confined to a small portion of the extended organism such as the palate or the nose in the body. Besides, as we should not forget either, the soul itself, in these stages, is merely an Aṇu a non-spatial point. These sensations therefore of taste and smell are at this stage as all filling and overwhelming as any other.

It is this idea which is technically put when it is said:

" From variety produced in the Rasa-tanmātra

there is produced Ap, that is, what is perceived as moist or liquid".

Finally, let us suppose that our experience of Odour-as-such is similarly and under similar circumstances changed into that of a variety of Odours. But the moment such a variety was perceived there would, as in the previous cases, be realised a consequent experience which must follow the perception as necessarily as the other consequent experiences following the perceptions of varieties in Sound, Feel, Colour and Flavour. And this consequent experience is, as a little reflection will show, neither that of all directions, that is Space, nor of Air, of Agni, the form-building energy, nor even of anything liquid—although these *may* all be there and indeed often are—but none of these need necessarily be present. The only experience which is absolutely necessary and is necessarily present is simply that a something is *standing* still or *staying* or *sticking*, namely, to or at the sense of smelling—therefore *standing* still on, or sticking to, the whole of *i. e.* all over, the soul, inasmuch as the sense of smell is at this stage all over the soul—as distinguished from the consequent experiences in the previous cases which are either all-directions, *i. e.*, Space, or *movements* of some sort. It is, in other words, an experience of something *stable*, *i. e.* of '*stability*' which is the essential characteristic of all things solid and may therefore be also spoken of as *solidity*. We may therefore say, that with the experience of variety in odours, there is also produced the experience of *something stable*, *i. e.*, of *stability* or *solidity*; and from solidity or stability again come all such experiences as hardness, roughness, pressure or weight and so on, *i. e.* what is meant by Pṛithivī in Sanskrit, (lit. Earth).

Or, as it may be stated in the technical language of the system:

From variety being produced in the Gandhatanmātra, there comes into manifestation the Pṛithivī, that is the

Principle of Stability and Solidity, or, which is the same thing, the stable or solid thing.

There is nothing absurd in this statement; for, as said above and as may be repeated once more, the sensation of the varieties of smell, as experienced by the Soul at this stage is, as it were, all over it and is as all-filling and overwhelming as any other.

Thus from the experiences of variety in the five general objects of perception there are produced also the five important factors or principles of experience, namely, Ākāsha or Etheriality, Vāyu or Aeriality, Agni or Formativity, Ap or Liquidity and Pṛithivī or Solidity; in other words, the ingredients of what we call the physical world (in so far as it is purely physical and actually experienced),—ingredients which are colletively called in Sanskrit by the technical name of the Bhūtas (lit. What have been, or happened, or the ever 'Have beens', and never 'Ares', or the Ghosts, namely, of the Real. [1]

The only thing which may perhaps be considered as not included in the above general facts is what is spoken of as Vitality or Life—that which builds up *organic* forms—which also is found manifest in the physical world. It is, however, not really omitted; for as we have seen that, from the highest and ultimate point of view, Prāṇa or vitality is only the Shiva Tattva which serves as the inner life of the universe as the Shakti, which produces all the diversity of forms. At a lower stage, as we have also seen, it is Ahaṅkāra which holds together organic forms and is therefore what appears as vitality or Prāṇa in the physical world. Leaving aside, then, the consideration of vitality or Prāṇa as a separate factor, which besides is hardly a *physical* element, we have in the ten classes of ingredients named above every thing of which the physical universe consists. For the latter,

---

1 For texts bearing on the production of these Bhūtas, see Appendix XII

as actually experienced, is, as can be easily shown, only an aggregate—in countless combinations and permutations—of

1. Varieties of Sound,
2. Varieties of Feel,
3. do of Colour (*i. e.*, Form),
4. do of Flavour,
and 5. do of Odour,

—things which are collectively called in Sanskrit the Vishayas, *i. e.*, 'objects' or what 'lies variously in front' and perceived as concomitant with, or, which is the same thing, as inherent in, the principles of the Ākāsha, Vāyu, Agni, Ap and Prithivī, that is, of Etheriality, Aeriality Formativity,[1] Liquidity and Solidity.

There is absolutely nothing else which is an ingredient of the physical universe, *as actually experienced*, which is not to be found included in these.

---

1. The term 'Formativity' might perhaps be substituted by 'Principle of Appearance' or 'Apparition' or even by 'Apparence' and 'Apparancy,' all of which words suggest the idea of vision, *i. e.*, of what is visible, as is implied by the Sanskrit word Rūpa. But as all these words have other connotations as well (as, for instance, in the phrase '*Appearance and Reality*' employed as the title of Bradley's well known work), it was thought best to use the term 'Formativity,' which, more than perhaps any other term, renders best the technical sense of the word 'Agni'.

'Agni' might be rendered as the 'Principle of *Expression*' as well, the word expression in this connection implying visible *Form* of course, as, for instance, in the phrase, the 'Expression' on one's countenance. This would also suggest the relation between Agni and Vāch or 'Speech',—a relation which is constantly referred to in the Upanishads and could be elaborated into a whole volume of essays. But inspite of this suggestion of the relation between Agni and Vāch, as conveyed in the word 'Expression', it had to be

And they come into manifestation from the Tanmātrās when varieties are produced in the latter.

SUMMARY AND CONCLUSION

These factors, as said above, are called the Tattvas, *i. e.*, the Principles into which the endless variety of things we experience, or can ever experience, can be reduced. They, in all possible combinations and permutations, make up the universe, physical and super-physical, that is, all actual or possible experience.

The Tattvas may, for the sake of convenience, be recapitulated here in the reverse order as follows:—

I. The five physical orders called the Bhūtas, namely, the principles of the experience of

1......*a*. Solidity (Pṛithivī),
2......*b*. Liquidity (Ap),
3......*c*. Formativity (Agni),
4......*d*. Aeriality (Vāyu),
5. and *e*. Etheriality (Ākāsha).

II. The five Powers or Capacities of activity called the Karmendriyas, namely, the capacities of

6......*a*. Resting and enjoying passively or re-creating (Upasthendriya),
7......*b*. Rejecting and discarding (Pāyvindriya),
8......*c*. Locomotion (Pādendriya),

---

avoided as a rendering of Agni, because of the ambiguity which attaches to it, equally as it does to the word 'Appearance' and its allied forms.

9......*d.* Handling, *i.e.*, operating as with the hands (Hastendriya),
10. and *e.* Voicing or expressing (Vāgindriya).

III. The five Generals of the Specific Sense-perceptions called the five Tanmātras, namely,

11......*a.* Odour-as-such (Gandha-Tanmātra),
12......*b.* Flavour-as-such (Rasa- do),
13......*c.* Colour-as-such (Rūpa- do),
14......*d.* Feel-as-such (Sparsha- do),
15. and *e.* Sound-as-such (Shabda-do).

IV. The five powers or Capacities of Perception called the five Buddhīndriyas or Jñānendriyas, namely, the powers of

16......*a.* Smelling (Ghrāṇendriya),
17......*b.* Tasting (Rasanendriya),
18......*c.* Seeing (Darshanendriya),
19......*d.* Feeling-by-touch (Sparshendriya),
20. and *e.* Hearing (Shravaṇendriya).

V. The three psychical or mental factors of

21......*a.* Manas
22......*b.* Ahaṅkāra
23. and *c.* Buddhi.

VI. 24. The Prakṛiti—that is, the general source of all the above, consisting of the three Affective Features of Sattva, Rajas, and Tamas, held in mutual neutralisation or equipoise.

VII. 25. The Puruṣha or the limited individual Spirit with its fivefold envelopment *i. e.*, the five Kañchukas, *viz:*

26......*a.* Kalā,
27......*b.* Vidyā,
28......*c.* Rāga,
29......*d.* Kāla,
30. and *e.* Niyati.

VIII. 31. Māyā—the producer of the Purusha and Prakṛiti.

IX. The three orders of the 'Pure Way' *viz:*

32......*a.* Sad-Vidyā or Shuddha-Vidyā,

33......*b.* Aishvarya or Īshvara Tattva,

34. and *c.* Sādākhya or Sadā-Shiva Tattva.

And X. The ever-existent, mutually inseparable realities of

35......*a.* the Shakti Tattva,

36. and *b.* the Shiva Tattva.

Or, in the order of what may be called, for want of a better phrase, their relative distances from the Ultimate Reality, that is, Parama Shiva, they are as follows:—

I. The ever-existing, mutually inseparable realities of

1.........*a.* the Shiva Tattva,

2... and *b.* the Shakti Tattva.

II. The three Orders of the, 'Pure Way', *viz:*

3......*a.* Sādākhya or Sadā-Shiva Tattva,

4......*b.* Aishvarya or Īshvara Tattva,

5. and *c.* Sad-Vidyā or Shuddha-Vidyā.

III. 6. Māyā—the producer of the Purusha and Prakṛiti.

IV. 7. The Purusha or the limited individual Spirit with its fivefold envelopment, or the five Kañchukas. *viz:*

8.......*a.* Niyati,

9.......*b.* Kāla,

10.......*c.* Rāga,

11......*d.* Vidyā,

12. and *e.* Kalā,

V. 13. The Prakṛiti—that is, the general source of all the five Kañchukas, as well as of all that follows,—consisting of the three Affective Features of Sattva, Rajas and Tamas, held in mutual neutralisation or equipoise.

VI. The three psychical or mental factors of

14.......*a.* Buddhi,
15.......*b.* Ahaṅkāra,
16. and *c.* Manas.

VII. The five Powers or Capacities of perception called the five Buddhīndriyas or Jñānendriyas, namely, the powers of

17........*a.* Hearing (Shravaṇendriya),
18........*b.* Feeling-by-touch (Sparshendriya),
19........*c.* Seeing (Darshanendriya),
20........*d.* Tasting (Rasanendriya),
21...and *e.* Smelling (Ghrāṇendriya).

VIII. The five Generals of the Specific Sense-perceptions called the five Tanmātras, namely,

22........*a.* Sound-as-such (Shabda-Tanmātra),
23........*b.* Feel-as-such (Sparsha- do),
24........*c.* Colour-as-Such (Rūpa- do),
25........*d.* Flavour-as-such (Rasa- do),
26...and *e.* Odour-as-such (Gandha- do).

IX. The five Powers or Capacities of activity called the Karmendriyas, namely, the capacities of

27.......*a.* Voicing or Expressing (Vāgindriya),
28........*b.* Handling *i. e.* operating as with the hands (Hastendriya),
29........*c.* Locomotion (Pādendriya),
30.......*d.* Rejecting and discarding (Pāyv-Indriya),
31...and *e.* Resting and enjoying passively or re-creating (Upasthendriya).

X. The five physical orders called the Bhūtas, namely, the principles of the experiences of

32........*a*. Etheriality (Ākāsha),
33........*b*. Aeriality (Vāyu),
34........*c*. Formativity (Agni),
35........*d*. Liquidity (Ap),
36..and *e*. Solidity (Pṛithivī).

Above and beyond them all, that is to say, transcending them all, and yet pervading and permeating them all, there stands Parama Shiva or Parā Saṁvit, the supremest Experience, beyond and unaffected by all time, space and relation, but yet alone making the existence of the manifested universe, constituted of the Tattvas, possible.

And this is so because the process whereby all this is produced is, as said at the very outset, not one of actual division, but one of logical thinking or experiencing out—that process of thought of which each successive step *pre-supposes* and *involves* the whole of the preceding ones, which also remain intact, though, it may be, quite in the back-ground.

And, therefore, what is true of Parama Shiva in this respect, is also true of every one of the Tattvas mentioned above in regard to the Tattvas which follow from it immediately or through the intervention of other Tattvas—a point which cannot be too strongly emphasised. That is to say, as Parama Shiva pervades all the Tattvas and the whole of the Universe, and yet remains for ever the same and unaffected by them, as it were standing beyond them all, transcending them all, so does each Tattva in regard to all the other Tattvas which succeed it. It pervades and permeates them all and yet remains ever the same—has still an existence of its own as it ever had, even after the Tattvas as its immediate and mediate products have come into manifestation.

But, as each preceding (*i. e.* previously manifested or experienced) Tattva, while remaining what it is, still permeates and pervades all the succeeding ones, it happens that there is present in each successive Tattva the whole of the preceding ones also. Each successively manifesting Tattva thus lives, moves, and has its entire being, as may be truly said, in the ones preceding it. That is to say, wherever there exists a lower Tattva, *i. e.*, a Tattva of greater restriction (being produced from one of a wider scope), there are also all the other and higher ones, in full manifestation and holding the lower, as it were, in their bosom, they existing as so many concentric circles of gradually decreasing extent—or, from another point of view, standing, like a number of mathematical points all occupying the same position and yet somehow maintaining their individuality, in the heart of the lower as its very life and soul. Thus the whole range of Tattvas are present in their entirety even in the lowest of them. In other words, the lowest Tattva *involves* all the higher ones as each successively lower Tattva involves the ones which precede it.

The process of the production of the Tattvas may, therefore, be spoken of, as it indeed is, as one of *involution*, the Reality or Parama Shiva being more and more involved, as, so to speak, it descends towards the stage at which it appears as the physical.

It is also a process—besides being one of logical experiencing out and of Involution—of differentiation, or rather, multiplication. For the Ultimate Reality, by repeatedly involving itself, produces not a single limited unit merely, but a multiplicity of such units. For, it will be remembered, that out of the thirty-six Tattvas enumerated in the list given above (p. 143), the first mentioned two main groups, *i. e.*, down to Sad-Vidyā (no. 5), are universal. Māyā also is Universal in a sense ; for there is only *one* and the same Māyā for all individual Puruṣhas, even though they may not, indeed do not, realise her as one and identical, in the same way as the Experiencers of the Pure Order realise their respective objects of experience in a given stage as one and identical in every respect.[1] But from the Purusha—with its fivefold Kañchuka or veil—downwards, the Tattvas are all limitedly individual; that is to say, they are not only many but mutually exclusive. Thus the product in the Purusha-Prakriti stage is not a Universal all-comprehending something or somethings but an infinite number of Purusha-Prakriti twins, which limit each other and are mutually exclusive. All the other products also, following the Purusha-Prakriti pairs, are similarly many, limited and mutually exclusive. Thus, there are produced, not a single triad of Buddhi, Ahaṅkāra and Manas, a single decad of Indriyas, and single quintad each of the Tanmātras and Bhūtas, but an endless number of triads, decads and quintads—as many as there are Purusha-Prakriti twins—which ultimately become involved *in* and *as* these subsequently produced Tattvas.

Finally, this countless number of individual, limited and mutually exclusive Buddhis, Ahaṅkāras and Manases, of the decads of the Indriyas and of the quintads of the Tanmātras and Bhūtas, are each an Aṇu, as the limited Purusha itself is an Aṇu, a non-spatial point, almost like a mathematical point. As each Purusha becomes more and more involved and ultimately results in the Bhūtas, and among them again in the Prithivī Tattva, what he really becomes—even though and while he remains what he as a Purusha is and what he as each of the intermediate links has become—is an Aṇu, namely an Aṇu of Prithivī.[2]

---

1. Māyā is one and identical for all Purushas in the same way as Prakriti, from the Sāṅkhya point of view, is one and identical for all Purushas as recognised by that system.

2. This stand-point of looking at the process of Universal manifestation, as leading to the production of Aṇus, has

Thus it happens that what are produced by this process of logical experiencing out and of involution and multiplication,—as its final results *in the direction* of involution and differentiation,—are an infinite number of Aṇus of the various classes of Tattvas, from the Purusha, wrapped in his fivefold Kañchuka, down to the Pṛithivī. And as they thus come into manifestation, they act and react on one another, producing a still further complication, of which the real nature will be considered a little later on. For our present purpose it will be enough just to note this fact, that, coming out into existence as so many classes of Aṇus, the Tattvas interact between themselves, and are each of them, for all practical purposes, so many separate and mutually exclusive limited entities.

This, however, is only one aspect of their existence—the distributive aspect. They have a collective existence as well and we have to note that fact too. In the collective aspect of their existence, each class of Tattvas forms a single unit, having an existence and behaviour of its own which are other than those of the distributive, *i. e.* separate, Tattvas of the class.

The idea may be illustrated by the example of the cells of a living body. There the cells have each an individual life and existence of its own, which for all practical purposes is independent of others and is self-contained. Yet they together form a single unit, a single living organism, which also has a definite life and existence of its own, not as a mere collection of many units, but as a single Unity, even though it is formed collectively by the aggregate of the individual cells.

---

reference to that particular means of realising the Divine State of Freedom or Mukti which is called Āṇavopāya in the Trika system, and which will be briefly explained later.

These collective entities are termed the Lords of the Tattvas, the Tattveshas or their Presiding Deities, Adhiṣhṭhātrī Devatās.

The more important of these collective entities or the Tattveshas are the following:—

1. Shrī-kaṇṭha or Shrī-Kaṇṭha-nātha in the Prakṛiti Tattva;

and 2. Brahmā in the region of the Physical Tattvas.[1]

Thus there are produced the Tattvas or the general factors, or principles constituting the Universe of experience, down to the world of solids, and thus do they exist as Aṇus as distributive entities, but as mighty beings as collective wholes. And all this is done by a process of logical Experiencing out and of *Involution* and differentiation.

And once this is done, the Divine Shakti, *i. e.*, the Universal Energy takes, as it were, an upward turn and begins to *evolve* and re-unite what has thus been involved and differentiated.

Before, however, going into a consideration, however briefly, of this question of Evolution, and leaving the subject of the Tattvas, let me just point out two very important facts in regard to them.

The first is that the Tattvas, as recognised by the Trika, are not mere philosophical abstractions which neither have any practical bearing on life nor are capable of realisation by most human beings. Their *rational comprehension* is no doubt not possible without philosophical reflection. But there is not *one* of us,—not even the least reflecting and most incapable of forming any intellectual comprehension of the Tattvas—who is

---

1. There are Tattveshas in the Pure Order also, but in a somewhat different sense. Who they are will be seen later.

not actually using them every moment of his life (even though he may not be aware of the fact), and is therefore not experiencing them *in a way*. Indeed, one is forced to experience them, however dimly and unthinkingly, inasmuch as they all stand as the permanent background and ever-present *pre-suppositions* of experience at every moment of one's life.

For instance, as I am writing this and occasionally looking out of my window, I am perceiving a brick building at a distance and a tall and fine date-palm tree waving in the wind, its leaves sounding pleasantly as they are moving. Now in this very perception even of these trivial things, I am experiencing, however dimly and implicitly, the existence of the whole series of the Tattvas. I am experiencing the Pṛithivī, Ap, Agni and Vāyu as Tattvas, in so far as I am thinking of the objects before me as solid, more or less moist—the tree having more moisture, *i. e.*, liquidity in it than the dry bricks of the building,—of both the objects as having forms and of the one as moving with a movement which I am *inferring* is *aerial* by having previous experience of aeriality, and of the other as not affected much by it.

I am experiencing Ākāsha as I am realising they are being perceived in a direction or directions, and as occupying and filling a certain area, of space, while there is 'Nothing' about them.

The existence of the Tanmātras is being realised, however vaguely and subconsciously, every moment I am referring the particular varieties of the Odour and Flavour (as I am thinking of the delicious fragrance and sweet taste of the fruit and of the sugary juice of the date palm, and am comparing them with the poverty of these in the building), of the Colour and Feel (the cool of the date leaves and their shade, however scanty, and the heat of the building as it *can* grow hot in the summer months in these parts of India[1]) and of the particular Sounds the waving date branches are making—I am referring these varieties to the general conceptions of Odour-, Flavour-, Colour-, Feel- and Sound-as-such, this reference alone enabling me to think of them as particulars, namely, the particulars of the Generals which the Tanmātras are.

The Indriyas are being realised as I am perceiving the tree and the building by means of the special senses of sight and hearing (the sound of the leaves) and symbolically speaking about them (for writing is nothing else) and am handling this pen.

I am experiencing the existence of Manas as a Tattva when I am selecting out of, *i. e.* to the exclusion of, a whole mass of other sensations, only a certain group, and am, with this selected group, picturing these objects, *i. e.* imaging them, in my *mind.* I am experiencing the Manas also when I am turning my attention now to the building and then to the tree and then again to the paper I am putting down my thoughts upon. Manas is being experienced also in the fact that the sense-perception of colours—the only one of the kind, excepting the occasional sound of the leaves, I am at present having of the tree and the building—is passing constantly away like the flow of a river and what I am really having, at every conceivable fraction of a second, is a fresh senastion of which the duration is far, far shorter than the sensation of the prick of a needle, and that, while this is what I am really receiving, I am still making, of what is only a series of *successive* points of sensation-pricks, a continuous whole, and realising it as a picture spread out in a space. (This however is not an actual experience but the result of psychological analysis).

1. The above was written at Jammu, the winter capital of His Highness the Mahārāja Sahib Bahadur of Jammu and Kashmir, a burningly hot place in the summer.

The existence of Ahaṅkāra is being recognised in the fact that, while I am actually perceiving only a colour-form spread out in space, I am substantiating this form by associating with it my *own* experiences of Solidity, Moisture, Odour, Flavour and the like—things which I am not now actually perceiving and which I am drawing from the store-house of my *own possessions* of previous experience: For what else is Ahaṅkāra but the totality of these possessions which alone give me my individual character as a particular person born and brought up in a particular country and surroundings?

The presence of the Buddhi is being realised in the fact that I am referring to a *general class* the picture, which is thus substantiated by associating with it other and previous experiences of *my own*; and as I am thinking of the one that it is a tree and of the other that it is a building, I am able to do so only bacause there already exists somewhere in the back-ground of my being and consciousness such an experience of the Generals. And Buddhi being none other than this experience of the Generals, I am realising Buddhi as I am making such a reference.

The existence of Prakṛiti is being recognised in the fact that while the perception of the tree with its waving leaves and branches against the lovely blue sky induces in me a *feeling of pleasure*, I am thinking how it would have induced me, if I were a child, to be so *active* as to climb up its scaly trunk for the fruit, and thus make me *suffer* all that *painful feeling* which such a procedure might involve; and how also the same very innocent looking tree could have been the occasion of throwing me, as such a fruit gathering child, into a state of *feeling stunned and senseless*, if, while plucking the fruit, I were struck heavily on the head by one of its waving branches or were stung by a swarm of hornets which not unoften build their nests on such trees. In other words, I am realising Prakṛiti as I am at present feeling pleasure at the sight of the tree—which feeling as I am realising it, is, as it were, welling up in me from a deeply buried source in my nature, and am also thinking how there are in me the potentialities of a moving pain and of a stunning feeling leading to immovability ; for Prakṛiti is no other than the Potentiality of these in me.

The Puruṣha is being recognised in what realises itself, however dimly, as the reality which, remaining motionless and changeless, and as it were, standing still somewhere in the back-ground of my being, witnesses, so to say from behind, the operations, *i. e.* the *movements* of the Senses, Manas, Ahaṅkāra and Buddhi as the tree is being perceived, and experiences the play of the Prakṛiti as the feelings, pleasant, painful or otherwise, which the perception of the tree is producing in me.

The Kañchukas of the Puruṣha are recognised in the fact that the Puruṣha, that is, myself as the ' witness ', feels itself limited as regards :—

a. Simultaneity of perception (Kāla)—the Puruṣha having such perception in succession only, now of the tree, now of the building and then again of the paper, desk and so on in the room in which I am writing;

b. Freedom as to where, how and what the Puruṣha should or should not experience, so that it is bound by certain restrictions of condition, of occasion, locality, cause and sequence,—it being obliged to perceive only the tree and the building here on this occasion as I am seated here and to be affected by them in a particular way or ways, so long there exist certain conditions (Niyati);

c. Interest, so that it can keep itself engaged in only a few things at a time (Rāga)—letting go its interest from the tree when engaged in writing down these thoughts, and being obliged to forego the latter task when comtemplating about the tree and the building;

d. The Sphere of its consciousness *i. e.*, its purview, so that it can have its perceptions (*i. e. visions* of the ideas or images as they are induced, or, as it is said, 'reflected', in the Buddhi) only within a restricted area (Vidyā)—it has perceptions of only what lies within a limited horizon, such as the date palm, the building, the walls of the room and a few other things; and

e. Power of accomplishment, so that it could not, even if it would, make or unmake the tree or the building as it is composing these lines as it pleases. (Kalā).

Māyā is being realised in the fact that, while what are being perceived as the tree and the building are really part and parcel of me, my own sensations and imaginations, substantiated by materials from my own Ahaṅkāra and pictured against the back-ground of my own Buddhi—which are really and finally but an aspect of myself——they are still being perceived as separated from me and from each other, one placed here and another there, "measured out" away from me and from each other.

So far, it is evident, the realisation of the Tattvas is direct in every individual human being, in the sense that they, coming into play, weave themselves into the experience which individuals, as limited and mutually exclusive beings, have in any given situation or sphere of existence. The realisation of the remaining Tattvas, from the Sad-Vidyā upwards to the Shiva Tattva, and beyond them still, the realistion of Parama Shiva, is not so direct. They are realised ordinarily, rather, as the most general and universal principles and presuppositions of experience, in such a way that these principles, when taken by themselves, would give to experience no individual colouring whatever, so as to make one set of experiences, in any given stage, in any way whatsoever different in content from any other set. That this is so will be quite evident if we have fully understood what has been said before regarding the nature of these higher Tattvas and of Parama Shiva. For it will then be seen that of these Tattvas:—

i. The Sad-Vidyā is really only a principle of correlation between the Experiencer and the Experienced as a universal whole—a something which holds these two aspects of Experience, as it were, in perfect equilibrium in which both are seen in equal prominence. Such a principle, it is obvious, is one and the same for all, but not limitedly individual in the same way as is, for instance, the Vidyā (one of the Kañchukas) or the Buddhi. My Vidyā or Buddhi is not the same as yours. For my Vidyā or Buddhi as an individual property enables me to have a set of experiences which is different in content from yours, and which as such excludes, to some extent at least, what is not mine but is yours. This could not be possible if your Vidyā or Buddhi were exactly one and the same thing with mine. For then there would be no reason why your Vidyā or Buddhi should give you an experience from any part of which I should be shut out by my Vidyā or Buddhi.

This is, however, not the case with the Sad-Vidyā which, as a general, *i. e.* universal, principle, only shows itself as the power which *equally* correlates both you and me as experiencers to what we both have as the experienced. Your relation, as the experiencer, to your own set of the experienced is no greater or no less—no more or no less strong—than my relation, in the same *kind* of capacity, to my set of the experienced. What therefore establishes this relation, both between you and your 'experienced' and between me and my 'experienced,' is really the same general or common thing or principle.

This being the nature of the principle of correlation between the Experiencer and the Experienced, *i. e.* of the Sad-Vidyā, it is very unlike the Vidyā or Buddhi which in you gives to you, let us say, a *wider* field of experience than the one in me does to me.

Similarly:—

ii. The Aishvara is really the Principle of *general* objectivity in which the subjectivity, or the 'I', is practically merged, *i. e.*, with which it is identified. And this general and universal principle of objectivity is *the same* in all, unlike the specific groups of objectivity which you and I, as limited and mutually exclusive individuals, experience;

iii. The Sādākhya is the *general* principle of Being without any individual colouring;

iv. The Shakti-Tattva is the general principle of Negation; and

v. The Shiva-Tattva is the general principle of the pure 'I', from which not only all individual colouring and all objectivity has been eliminated, but in which the very notion of Being, as implied in 'am', has been suppressed; while

vi. Parama Shiva is that Reality which is the most *Supremely Universal,* and but for which neither the Negation of the 'Am' and of all objectivity, nor their subsequent emergence into view can have any meaning. Leave out Parama Shiva as the most Supremely Universal Reality, and there would be no more meaning in the appearance and existence of the Tattvas than there would be in the evolution and existence of the 'ions', and then of the atoms, as recognised by Western Chemistry, if the existence of the Universal Ether were denied. It has been made clear, I hope, that the appearance and existence of the Tattvas are as necessary for experience, (or, which is the same thing, for the existence of the

Universe) as the 'ions' and 'atoms' are for the existence of things physical; and the same logic which demands the recognition of a Universal Ether in the case of the latter demands also the recognition of Parama Shiva in regard to the former.

And if we understand in this way the true nature of the Tattvas from the Sad-Vidyā upwards and of Parama Shiva, we shall also see how even these Tattvas and Parama Shiva are realised *in a way* (though not certainly like the other Tattvas) in every experience, however trival. For then we see how :—

The presence of the Sad-Vidyā is to be recognised in the fact that there is a correlation between the perception of the tree and the building on the one hand and myself on the other—the correlation of subject and object, of the Experiencer on the one hand, and, of the Experienced on the other, as distinguished from all means of experience such as the Senses, Manas, Ahaṅkāra and the Buddhi. There is no reason why or how this correlation between two such diametrically opposed groups should ever be established, if there were not in me something of which the Experiencer in me on the one hand and the Experienced, on the other, are the two factors or sides which are already thus united as one correlated whole and yet are distinct, *i. e. differentiated,* facts so as to be recognised as two. This something is the Sad-Vidyā.

The presence of the Aishvara is similarly to be recognized in that *of which* these two are the aspects so correlated by the Sad-Vidyā and *in which* the aspects must already exist as an *undifferentiated whole,* the one *i. e.* the subject, the 'I', being merged into the other.

The Sādākhya is also there inasmuch as, while I am perceiving the tree and the building, I am not only realising, however subconsciously, that I am myself a 'Being', a changeless reality which always *is,* but I am also thinking of the tree and the building, as somethings which *are*—

that is, I am thinking that there is in them a something which is *real and changeless* or indestructible. This idea of Being which I am associating with the perceptions of the tree and the building can never be got anywhere in the world of sense perception, where all things are fleeting and constantly changing, and therefore is not *born* of an experience which is to be found stored up in the Ahaṅkāra. It is therefore already and always existing in me as the notion of being, that is as one of the most general of all conceptions; and as such constitutes the Sādākhya.

Then again there can be recognised the presence of both the Shakti and Shiva Tattvas in me—rather my existence in them—inasmuch as there is and must be the experience of the pure 'I,' apart even from the experience of the simple 'I *am*', *i. e.*, of Being. For the experience of 'I am' or of Being is constantly presupposing the experience of the pure 'I', without the relation which is implied in the copula 'am.' But it could not be thus *presupposed* if it were not already there in me. And because the Shiva Tattva is none other than this pure 'I', which is without even a thought of an 'am', therefore every moment the pure 'I' is being presupposed, the Shiva Tattva is being realised, however dimly and vaguely, in experience. And if there is the presence of the pure 'I' in me—or rather of the 'me' in the pure 'I'—there must exist in me also that which '*Negates*' the experience of the 'am'. And it is this Negating Power which is the Shakti Tattva in me.

Finally, because the pure 'I' of the Shiva Tattva and the Negative Power of the Shakti Tattva cannot but be the two aspects of one and the same thing,—from which they can never be dissociated, any more than they can be dissociated from each other, each being related to the other as *Power* to the Powerful,—therefore *that* Something of which they are but aspects must also be there in me, *i. e.*, behind and permeating all that I experience as my personal being, as well as all the objects and means of experience. It is this Something which is the Parama Shiva in me.

Thus it is that all the Tattvas are not only always present in me, and 'I', as a limited person, am present in the higher ones of them, but every one of them is actively participating in very experience I am having—even such a trivial experience as the perception of a tree and a building which I am looking at out of my window.

The Tattvas are, therefore, being realised, most dimly no doubt, at every moment of our lives, even by those of us who can hardly form any clear and rational idea of them.

They are being realised, that is, as they are acting as the guiding and determining principles and essential factors of our every-day experience; namely in the following way:—

1. The Pṛithivī, Ap, Agni, Vāyu and the Ākāsha Tattvas are acting as the general experiences, respectively, of all Solidity, Liquidity, the merely chemical form-building Energy, Aeriality and Directions or empty Space; while the Tanmātras are acting as the general experiences of Odour, Flavour, Colour, Feel-by-touch and Sound as such:—these two groups serving constantly as the principles and essential elements of all our purely physical experiences.

2. The ten Indriyas—the five powers of Perception and five powers of Action—are acting as the principles and essential elements of all our sense organs and active muscles of the body.

3. The Manas, Ahaṅkāra and Buddhi are working as the principles and essential means of all the mental and psychical experiences on the part of the individual soul.

4. The Prakṛiti is manifesting herself as that principle in us which, as the deeply buried and hidden source and fountain of all feelings—pleasure, pain and callousness—is constantly welling up in one or other of these forms as the individual soul is having its physical and psychical experiences.

5. The Purushha is acting as that principle in our daily life which—standing as it were in the back-ground of the Indriyas, Manas, Ahaṅkāra and Buddhi and face to face with Prakṛiti—realises itself as the subject which is being affected by these experiences, *i. e.*, which is either enjoying them, suffering from them or is being so struck down by them as to become insensible; in other words, which is being affected by these three types of the modifications of the Prakṛiti.

6. The five Kañchukas are acting constantly as those limitations in us which characterise the soul as an individual and limited entity, and which are inseparably *sticking to it*, all the time it is having experiences as a limited subject, and without which it can, as such a limited subject, never have any experiences whatsoever.[1]

---

1 एते च प्रमातृलग्नतयैव भान्ति (*Īsh. Prat. Vim.*, III. i. 9.)—' They appear as *sticking* to the Experiencer'. That is to say, the Experiencer, as a limited individual subject of experience, has these always with it, covering it, as it were, with a manifold veil, through which alone it can ever have experience. This veil for ever interposes itself between the Experiencer on the one hand and the Experienced on the other. In other words, in all limited experience, the veil is for ever presupposed, it being there first as an inevitable pre-requisite before any limitedly individual experience is had.

If this nature of the Kañchukas is properly understood, they will then be seen to be *essentially* what Kant called ' the Forms of perception and conception ' which, like the Kañchukas, are always with the experiencing subject, as the inevitable presuppositions and indispensably pre-requisite

7. Māyā is being realised inasmuch as she acts as the principle which imposes these limitations on what is really and essentially unlimited by either Time, Space or Form, and as that which makes one realise a separation between himself as the Experiencer and the objects which are experienced and thus serves as the cause of experiencing a plurality where there is really none.

8. The Sad-Vidyā is acting as the Principle of correlation between the Experiencer and the Experienced, which would otherwise not only remain unconnected with each other, but there would be no reason whatsoever why what are mutually so different in nature, as are the Experiencer and the Experienced, should be able to affect each other at all; or there should be any knowledge and experience at all.

9. The Aishavara is acting, if such a term can at all be used in connection with this and the following Tattvas, as the Principle in which the Experiencer and the

---

conditions of experience. Indeed Kant's 'Forms of perception and conception' would seem to agree with the Kañchukas of the Trika philosopher not only in essence but, to a great extent, in details also. For instance, the (a) Time and (b) Space and Causality of Kant are nothing but the (a) Kāla and (b) Niyati of the Trika.

Thus it would seem that this 'discovery' of Kant had already been known in India many centuries before that great German was born. Yet it is this discovery of the 'Forms of perception and conception' which is one of the principal achievements that made Kant's name so great in the West. But how many are there, even in India, who have ever heard of the poor Brāhman philosophers of Kashmir who knew these very things, and much more, not only in general outlines but in detail, long before Kant's time? Most deplorable indeed is the degradation of Indians who must import from Europe even things philosophical, wherein at any rate their ancestors excelled so greatly.

Experienced, when so correlated, stand unified; for what are thus correlated, like the two poles of a magnet, imply an essence of which, as a unity, they are the poles.

10. The Sādākhya is serving as the principle which enables any of us to experience, *i. e.*, to feel, think and speak of, anything, including oneself as an individual, as a Being.

11. The Shiva Tattva is showing itself as the Principle of the pure 'I' as distinguished from the personal Ego of the Ahaṅkāra; while the Shakti Tattva is being realised as the Principle which divests the Shiva Tattva of everything else, so that it can become the principle of the pure 'I'.

12. While these Tattvas are thus constantly acting and showing themselves as the Principles and essential and general factors of our daily and hourly experiences—which are but the various combinations of these principles and elements—the Parama Shiva stands behind and beyond them all, as well as comprising them all, as their one and supremest Synthesis.

The second fact which I should point out about the Tattvas, before leaving them to consider other topics of the Trika, is that, if the Tattvas and Parama Shiva are thus always with every one of us, nay if we are every one of us in them and made up of them, and if, on that account, we are constantly realising them, though only in a dim and vaguely abstract fashion, without ever, or hardly ever, being able to imagine their real grandeur and sway, this is not the only way in which they are realised, or that there is no other means by which their full sway and true grandeur can be experienced. On the contrary, there certainly is such a means. This means consists in that method of self-culture, mental, moral, spiritual and even physical, which constitutes what is called Yoga, in the true sense of the term, and which enables a Spirit to shake off the very limitations that make of the real Experiencer such a limited entity and to rise to those regions of experience which the highest Tattvas are. Those who train themselves by this method of Yoga, and who are therefore called Yogins, can and do realise the Tattvas by direct experience as clearly as, indeed more clearly than, we perceive the physical and sense-objects; and as they thus realise them, they experience the Tattvas in their real nature and grandeur which we, considering them but rationally, can only dimly guess, arguing in our minds, how each successively higher synthesis (as the higher Tattavs are of the lower ones, and as a Tattva is of the particulars of a class) must be ever increasingly more, and not *less*, grand and glorious, than the physical universe in all its grandeur can ever be, and how it must be far otherwise than the bare abstraction which a Tattva, when merely infrentially conceived as a principle, appears to be.

Indeed it is thus,—so the Hindu Philosopher emphatically declares,—by means of Yoga-experience, that the Tattvas and their true nature first came to be known and taught; and not by mere logical inference. Logic and reasoning were applied to them only after they had thus been realised by direct experience, in order just to show how their existence and reality can also be rationally established, and how they *need not and should not be taken as mere matters of faith or revelation.*

However that may be, the point which should be noted here is that the Tattvas are regarded not as mere philosophical abstractions and logical inferences from the ordinary sensible and physical experiences of human beings *as limited individuals.* They are, on the contrary, realities which can, while as the principles of our daily experience they are present with us at every moment of our lives, be realised in all their grandeur and glory, in and as direct and positive experience, by that self-unfoldment to which true Yoga leads.

While the Tattvas, as both the guiding principles

and the constitutive factors in the daily lives of every one of us, are thus participating in every experience, however trivial, which every one of us is having at every moment of his life, they are not, *from the Puruṣha with his five Kañchukas downward,* the same for every limited and individual experiencer—a fact which has been pointed ont before and which may be repeated here. They are, on the contrary, different for different experiencing entities, each experiencing entity having, so to say, its own set or series of the Tattvas. They are no doubt *alike,* so that one set may be spoken of as the *same* as any other set, in the same sense that the repeated performances of a dramatic piece, *i. e.,* a set or series of dramatic actions, songs, and the like, by a particular dramatic company, are spoken of as the same performance, although as a matter of fact they are but performances which are really all different, although *quite alike* one to the other. In the case of the Tattvas, both as the principles of experience on the part of the different limited souls as well as such *experiences* themselves on their part, considered as so many separate but similar performances, the one performing company, to borrow a simile from the Sāṅkhya, is Māyā.[1] It is one and the same Māyā which, while she ever remains what she is, gives for each limited Puruṣha, a separate performance. Each such performance given separately for each Puruṣha constiutes both the principles of experiences and the experiences themselves, on the part of that particular

---

1. From the Sāṅkya point of view the one performing company is the Prakṛiti which is one for all the Puruṣhas.

In this case the simile has a better application inasmuch as the three Guṇas of Sattva, Rajas and Tamas, which, when in equipoise, constitute the Prakṛiti, may be conceived as the partners in the performing company. From the Trika point of view the better simile would perhaps be that of a Magician to whom Māyā may be likened.

Purushа, because the experiences are only the various combinations, permutations and differentiations, of the principles. Such a performance constitutes, in other words, what really and literally is the Universe of that particular Purusha as a *limited being.* And because these separate performances for separate Purushas are, under similar circumstances, so much *alike*—given as they are by the same company of Māyā—they are mistaken for a single performance. Thus it comes to be believed that it is a single universe that we all, as limited beings, experience, while as a matter of fact everyone of us has a separate and distinct universe of his own[1].

And if with all the obvious and well-known differences in the contents of our several experiences as mutually exclusive and limited beings, we can still think and speak as the *same* of these contents, *i. e.,* of our various universes, which are none other than these several sets of the contents of the several experiences on our part, it goes without saying that the experiencers of the Pure Order experience a universe which is quite *identical.* For, as we shall see later, there too is, in a sense, a plurality of experiencers, though there is absolutely no difference in the contents of their several experiences.

Even then, what they experience severally is not one but several, though absolutely identical, performances—in the sense that these are absolutely alike in all and every

1. The 'universe' which each limited individual experiences is really his own, and is, as such, quite other than, even though it may be quite similar to, that of another, *in the same way* as the vision of one eye is different from that of the other. As is well known, one sees with one's two eyes not *one* and the same picture of a thing, but *two* pictures, which are no doubt quite alike. The individual *experiences* of the universe (or, which is the samething the universe itself), is called, for this reason, Prātisvika in Sanskrit, *i. e. 'each one's own.'* But this does not mean solipsism ; see Appendix XII.

respect. And the one performing company in their case is the Divine Shakti as such—She who holds in her womb the whole of the Universe, both of the Pure and Impure Orders, as an eternal potentiality, and goes on reproducing it eternally and severally for the several experiencers, so long as there are any in manifestation.

But although the Tattvas and Universes as experiences are thus different for different experiencers, they in each stage yet form a unity—have, as said above, a collective existence which behaves as, and constitutes, as a matter of fact, a single entity—as ultimately the whole is a single unity in and as Parama Shiva. That is to say, the Tattvas have both a distributive and a collective existence—the former as many units and the latter as a single unit.

And as the experiencers have a collective existence, their 'universes' also have similar existences forming the experiences of the collective entities at the different stages. But while such distributively and collectively existing universes must be very different in the region where limited beings have distributive experiences, there can be hardly any such differences where the experience is not limited but universal, being constituted of every thing there is to experience at any given stage, and without any restriction as to duration and extension, *i. e.*, is timeless and spaceless.

Part II

History and Literature

The first beginnings of what has been called 'Kashmir Shaivaism', to distinguish it from other forms of Shaivaism known and still practised in different parts of India, may have to be traced to the *Shiva Sūtras*[1], which, together with the commentary on them by Kṣhemarāja called the *Vimarshinī*, have been published as the opening volume of this series of publications, *i. e. The Kashmir Series of Texts and Studies.* Its teachings and practices are given, in the literature of the system, the distinctive name of *Trika-shāsana, Trika-shāstra* or simply *Trika*[2]; and are often referred to as the

1. Dr. Bühler (*Report* pp. 78 & clxvii) calls them the '*Spanda Sūtras*' which however is a mistake. The name *Spanda Sūtras* is given to the *Spanda-Kārikās*, see below p. 15. That by the *Shiva Sūtras*, the Sūtras published in the first volume of this series are meant may be seen from the *Shiva Sūtra Vārttika* where the Sūtras are often introduced with the words 'शिवः सूत्रमरीरचत्' or 'सूत्रमाह महेश्वरः'. The *Spanda Pradīpikā* (on Kārikā 11) and the *Tantrāloka* (Ahn. i. p. 40 of MS.), among others, also refer to them as the *Shiva Sūtras*.

2. Even षडर्धक्रमशास्त्र, see *Tantra-Sāra*, Ahn. ix (beginning); also षडर्धक्रमविज्ञान, *Tantrāl. Viv.* i. 9. The word Trika refers, among other things, to the triple principle with which the system deals, *viz.* शिव-शक्ति-अणु or पति-पाश-पशु. The phrase नर-शक्ति-शिवात्मकं त्रिकं occurs in the *Parā Triṁ. Viv.* Intro. Verse. 3.

Rahasya-Sampradāya[1], while Shaivaism in general is spoken of as *Shiva-Shāsana*[2] or *Shivāgama*.

The peculiarity of the Trika consists in the fact that, as a system of Philosophy, it is a type of idealistic monism (advaita)[3], and as such differs in fundamental

---

1. The occasional reference to the system as त्रैयम्बकसंप्रदाय is due probably to the fact that Somānanda, the promulgator of its *philosophy*, as distinguished from its doctrines as a system of *faith*, (see below p. 26) claimed his descent from त्र्यम्बक.

For all these various names given to the system see, among others, *Parā Triṁ. Viv.*, Fols. 199 and 205; *Tantrāl. Viv.*, Ahn. i. p. 34 and *Shiva-Sū. Vim.* पृ० २.

2. 'ज्ञानाज्ञानस्वरूपं यदुक्तं प्रत्येकमप्यदः ।
द्विधा पौरुषबौद्धत्वविधोक्तं शिवशासने ॥' *Tantrāl.* i. p. 49.

Here शिवशासने is explained by the commentator as पञ्चस्रोतोरूपे पारमेश्वरे दर्शने. From this it is clear that शिवशासन means Shaivaism or Shaiva Philosophy *in general* because the special Kashmiri form or Trika is regarded as not पञ्चस्रोतोरूप but only ऊर्ध्वस्रोतोरूप; see below p. 6, note 1.

3. See below Part II.

As an example of its thorough-going Advaitism the opening stanza of the *Shiva Dṛiṣhti* of Somānanda may be quoted. It runs as below:—

असद्रूपसमाविष्टः स्वात्मनात्मनिवारणे ।
शिवः करोतु निजया नमः शक्त्या ततात्मने ॥

Here the worshipper as well as the obstacles for the removal of which the worship is offered (आत्मनिवारणे *i. e.* आत्मस्वरूपभूतानां विघ्नानां प्रतिविधानार्थम्) are regarded as essentially the same as Shiva himself. Such being the teaching of the Trika Shāstra, which includes, as will be seen (below p. 7), the Spanda Shāstra, the identification of the latter with what is termed 'Shaiva Darshana' in the *Sarva Darshana Saṅgraha* of Mādhavāchārya, as was done by Dr. Bühler, is evidently a mistake. As a matter of fact, Kashmir Shaivaism or the Trika, is treated in that work under the name of Pratyabhijñā Darshana. That Mādhavāchārya was right in this will be shown later (below pp. 17-20). See also *Bhandarkar*, page 81.

principles from other forms of Shaiva Philosophy, for instance, from what is described under the name of the Shaiva Darshana in the *Sarva-Darshana-Saṅgraha* of Mādhavāchārya.

Although the Trika form of Shaivaism would seem to have made its first appearance in Kashmir at the beginning of the ninth, or perhaps towards the end of the eighth century of the Christian era,[1] Shiva Shāsana or Shivāgama, that is Shaivaism as such, is far older than this date.[2] Indeed we may have to trace its beginnings in the Vedic Revelations. In Kashmir itself—where even the most orthodox followers of the Shivāgama admit that the Trika-Shāsana first appeared (or, as they put it, *re*appeared) about the beginning of the ninth Christian century—Shivāgama is regarded as of high antiquity, indeed of eternal existence like the Vedas. According to the belief and tradition of the Kashmir Shaivas, the history of Shivāgama and of the Trika is as follows:—

" Before their manifestation, all Shāstras, which are but thoughts expressed as speech, like the manifested

---

1. Below p. 23.
2. *Bhandarkar* p. 76.

It would be most interesting to trace the history of Shaivaism in general from its very beginning, which is most likely to be found outside the valley of Kashmir, and of its subsequent spread from the valley under the form of the Trika, specially as this investigation has now been started by the papers of Mr. D. R. Bhandarkar (paper on *Lakulīsha*) and Drs. Fleet (*J. R. A. S.* for 1907, pp. 419 et seqq.) and Barnett (*Siddhānta Dīpikā*, Vol. xi, pp. 62-64 and 101-103 and *J. R. A. S.* for 1910, p. 706). But I had to give up this attempt, which, with great diffidence no doubt, I once thought of undertaking, for two reasons: the great difficulty in getting (situated as I am in Kashmir) necessary works for study and reference and the consideration that the result of such an investigation could not very well be incorporated in what was to be merely an introduction to a text, without making the publication inordinately bulky, but should be published separately as an independent volume.

universe itself which forms the object of that thought and speech, existed in the as yet unuttered thought and experience of the Supreme Deity in the form of the 'All-transcending Word' (the Parā Vāk) that is beyond all objective thought and speech in every one of their forms, not excepting even the Avyakta, the most germinal of them.

" Next, as the manifestation of the Universe begins, the Parā Vāk, the All–transcending Word, also begins to appear in the form of that thought and experience which would hold, as it were in a mighty Vision, the whole universe which is to be and which is still in a most germinal and undifferentiated state so that it cannot yet be thought, much less spoken, of as consisting of 'this' or 'that'——the Parā Vāk puts forth, in other words, another form, that of the Pashyantī, which is the 'Vision'[1] of the whole Universe in its undifferentiated form. Then as the manifestation of the Universe progresses, and its contents form the objects of discursive thought and experience—as they become distinguishable from one another as 'this' or 'that',—what was erstwhile the all-holding 'field of Vision,' the Pashyantī Vāk, assumes a third form, the *Middle* one, Madhyamā, which stands, as it were as a link, between, on the one hand, the undifferentiated Pashyantī and, on the other, what is soon going to be the spoken word, the Vaikharī Vāk[2], which is

---

1. '……पश्यन्ती दर्शनात्मिका ।' *Shiva Dṛiṣh.*, ii. 35.

See also Utpala's *Comm.* on *Shiva Dṛiṣh.*, ii. 1 and 3. Comp. also the Greek philosophical conception of the 'Idea.'

2. i. विभक्तककारादिवर्णरूपा वैखरी वर्ण्यते । Utpala's *Ṭīkā* on *Shiva Dṛiṣh.* ii. 7, where the following is also quoted

स्थानेषु विवृते वायौ कृतवर्णपरिग्रहा ।
वैखरी वाक् प्रयोक्तॄणां प्राणवृत्तिनिबन्धना ॥

ii. विखरे शरीरे भवत्वात् वैखरी; *Tantrāl. Viv.* iii. p. 136.

The explanation of वैखरी, however, given by the commentator on the *Alaṅkāra-Kaustubha*, would seem to indicate that he derived it from ख्र or ख्रु (as preserved in विख्र and विख्रु) meaning the nose, or rather, the vocal organ.

but thought and experience expressed by means of the vocal organ. And what are called the Shaiva Shāstras—indeed all Shāstras—are nothing but this Divine Madhyamā Vāk assuming these forms and 'flowing out,' as the Vaikharī or spoken words, in five 'streams,' from what may be regarded as the 'Five Faces' of the Deity,—the Faces which represent the five aspects of His five-fold power and glory—namely, of Chit, Ānanda, Ichchhā, Jñāna and Kriyā[1], and which are respectively called Īshāna, Tat-Purusha Sadyojāta, Aghora and Vāma. The Shaiva Shāstras, which thus streamed forth from the five Divine Mouths in these the five-fold faces of the Deity, consisted originally and in their entirety of no less than sixty-four 'systems' representing as many aspects of thought and suited to the diverse needs of the people but were all divisible under the three classes of what taught

" *a.* the essential unity and identity of all that appears as the many; (Advaita or Abheda);

"*b.* the diversity of principles which, in this way only *i. e.* as a diversity, could be comprehended by some as the essence of things (Bheda); and

"*c.* the unity, from one point of view, and diversity from another, of these principles according to the comprehension of others (Bhedābheda).[2]

"But of these sixty four systems, which, as such, at first appeared in the form of the Madhyamā Vāk of the Deity and afterwards 'streamed forth' from his five Divine Mouths, as Vaikharī the Spoken words, but which had all along existed, first as the Parā and then in the Pashyantī form—of these sixty-four Shaiva Shāstras most disappeared with the growing influence of the Kali age and with the gradual disappearance of the Ṛiṣhis who, having learnt the Shāstras, were the repositories of their knowledge. As, thus, with the disappearance of the Shāstras the world

1. For the meanings of these technical terms, which are left purposely untranslated here, see below Part II.

2. See my *Hindu Realism*, Introduction, Section on the meaning of Prasthāna-bheda, pp. 5–10.

became engrossed in spiritual darkness, Shiva,—as the Deity is called,—took pity on men and, appearing on the Kailāsa mountain in the form of Shrīkaṇṭha, commanded the Sage Durvāsas to spread in the world the knowledge of these Shāstras again. Durvāsas, thus commanded, created, by the power of his mind, three sons,—Tryambaka, Āmardaka and Shrīnātha by names—whom he chraged with the mission of establishing spiritual order and of teaching men again the ancient and eternal Shaiva faith and doctrine in their three aspects of Abheda, Bheda and Bhedābheda—of Unity, Diversity and Diversity-in-unity,—Tryambaka was to teach the first, Āmardaka the second, while Shrīnātha was to have the charge of the last. It is this Abheda or Advaya Shaiva teaching, thus retaught to the world by Tryambaka, which is spoken of as the Trika."[1]

1. The above is freely translated from the following account summarised from the *Tantrāloka* and its *Commentary.*

इह खलु परपरामर्शसारबोधात्मिकायां परस्यां वाचि सर्वभावनिर्भरत्वात् सर्वं शास्त्रं परबोधात्मकतयैव उज्जृम्भमाणं सत्, पश्यन्तीदशायां वाच्यवाचकाविभागस्वभावत्वेन असाधारणतया अहंप्रत्यवमर्शात्मकमन्तरुदेति; अत एव हि तत्र प्रत्यवमर्शकेन प्रमात्रा परामृश्यमानो वाच्योऽर्थोऽहन्ताच्छादित एव स्फुरति; तदनु तदेव मध्यमाभूमिकायामन्तरेव वेद्यवेदकप्रपञ्चोदयात् भिन्नभिन्नवाच्यवाचकस्वभावतया उल्लसति। तत्र हि परमेश्वर एव चिद्-आनन्द-इच्छा-ज्ञान-क्रियात्मकवक्त्रपञ्चकासूत्रणेन सदाशिवेश्वरदशामधिशयानः तद्वक्त्रपञ्चकमेलनया पञ्चस्रोतोमयम् अभेद-भेदाभेद-भेददशोट्टङ्कनेन तत्तद्भेद-प्रभेदवैचित्र्यात्म निखिलं शास्त्रमवतारयति यत् बहिः वैखरीदशायां स्फुटतामियात्।

तथा हि प्रथममेव ईशान-तत्पुरुष-सद्योजात-अघोर-वामाख्यं वक्त्रपञ्चकमाविरभूत्; तेभ्य एव प्रत्येकं मुखेभ्यः चतुष्षष्टितन्त्राणि शैवदर्शनानि जज्ञिरे। तानि कलिकालुष्यात् उपदेष्टृजन-परम्परान्तधानवशात् विच्छिन्नसंचाराणि व्यनश्यन्। इत्थं व्युच्छिन्ने शिवशासने कदाचित् कैलासगिरौ परिभ्रमन् श्रीकण्ठमूर्तिः शिवो विच्छिन्नस्य निखिलशैवशास्त्रोपनिषत्सारभूतस्य षडर्धक्रम-(त्रिकमत-) विज्ञानस्य प्रचारार्थं दुर्वाससं मुनिमाजिज्ञपत्। स मुनिः मानसान् सिद्धान् (त्र्यम्बक-आमर्दक-श्रीनाथाख्यान्) अद्वय-द्वय-द्वयाद्वयमतव्याख्यातॄन् मठिकासु सत्संप्रदायमार्गं प्रचारयितुं न्ययुङ्क्त। तेषु मतेषु प्रशस्तम् अद्वयार्थविषयकं त्रिकाख्यमतं त्रैयम्बकसंप्रदायकं सर्वश्रेष्ठं प्रशस्यते; यदुक्तम्

वेदाच्छैवं ततो वामं ततो दक्षं ततः कुलम्।
ततो मतं ततश्चापि त्रिकं सर्वोत्तमं परम्॥ [तन्त्रालो० टी० ३४ पृ०]

इति; अनेन सर्वस्रोतोमुखेभ्यः समुत्पन्नानां शैवतन्त्राणां मध्ये ऊर्ध्वस्रोतःप्रसृतस्य अस्यैव सर्वोत्तमत्वात्।

A portion of this account is given in brief in the extract made from the now lost *Shiva Driṣhṭi Vṛitti*; see below page 24.

However this may be, before tracing the history of the Trika as represented in its existing literature, since its appearance—or *re*appearance according to the belief of its followers—in the 9th. Christian Century, it may be convenient to give here a brief account of this literature itself.

The literature of the Trika falls into three broad divisions:—

A. THE ĀGAMA-SHĀSTRA,

B. THE SPANDA-SHĀSTRA.

and C. THE PRATYABHIJÑĀ-SHĀSTRA.[1]

The chief features of the three Shāstras, as they are called, and a few of the principal and still existing works belonging to each of them are as follows:—

A. THE ĀGAMA-SHĀSTRA—This is regarded as of superhuman authorship. It lays down both the

---

1. Bühler's statement (*Report* pp. 78 & 79) that the Spanda and the Pratyabhijñā Shāstras are two different systems of philosophy was based on an error. See below pp. 17–33. The term शास्त्र as employed in this connection does not mean a separate system but a treatise or treatises dealing with a particular aspect or aspects of the same system; comp., for instance, श्रीमालिनीविजयोत्तर-सिद्धातन्त्र-स्वच्छन्दादिशास्त्रेषु; *Parā, Trim. Viv.*, fol. 73 क. As is well known, these works do not represent so many different *systems* but only *treatises* on the various aspects of the same system of thought, namely, the Trika. That on the Trika there were many treatises each of which was called a शास्त्र may be gathered also from the following,

श्लैरेकोनविंशत्या त्रिंशिकेयं विवेचिता ।

सर्वेषु त्रिकशास्त्रेषु ग्रन्थीर्निर्दलयिष्यति ॥ *Parā Trim. Viv.*, last verse. Com. also the phrase शिवदृष्टिशास्त्र in *Parā Trim. Viv.* fol. 124 क. If by शास्त्र we are to understand a separate system of philosophy, then the शिवदृष्टिशास्त्र must also be regarded as different from the प्रत्यभिज्ञाशास्त्र. We, however, know that this is not only not the case but that the latter is only 'a reflection' (प्रतिबिम्बक) of the former; *Īshv. Pra. Vim.*; Intro. verse 2.

doctrines (jñāna) and the practices (kriyā) of the system *as revelations* which are believed to have come down (āgama) through the ages, being handed down from teacher to pupil.

Among the works (if they may be so called) belonging to this Shāstra there is a number of Tantras, of which the chief ones are the following:—

Mālinī Vijaya (or *Mālinī Vijayottara*)
Svachchhanda
Vijñāna Bhairava
Uchchhuṣhma Bhairava
Ānanda Bhairava (lost)
Mṛigendra
Mataṅga
Netra
Naishvāsa
Svāyambhuva
Rudra-yāmala (from which the famous *Parā-Triṁshikā* verses are said to be taken)

Most of these had existed long before the appearance (or *re*appearance) of the Trika and taught mostly a dualistic doctrine; at any rate they seem to have been interpretated in a dualistic, even a pluralistic, sense.[1]

It was to stop the spread of this dualistic teaching[2] and to show that the highest form of the Shivāgama taught only the pure Advaita Tattva—Idealistic Monism—that there were revealed the

Shiva Sūtras,

which therefore form, from the Trika point of view, the most important part of the Āgama Shāstra. Indeed, they are spoken of as the 'Shivopaniṣhat-Saṅgraha'[3] which is again interpreted as 'Shivarahasyāgama-Shāstra-Saṅgraha'.

---

1. Below p. 10.
2. द्वैतदर्शनाधिवासितप्राये जीवलोके रहस्यसंप्रदायो मा विच्छेदि-इत्याशयतः
Shiv. Sū. Vim. पृ० २.
3. *Shiv. Sū. Vim.* पृ० ३ and foot-note 14 on it.

Their authorship is attributed to Shiva himself,[1] while they are said to have been revealed to the sage Vasugupta who must have lived towards the end of the eighth or the beginning of the ninth Christian century.[2]

On the *Shiva Sūtras* there are:—

a. The *Vṛitti*
b. The *Vārttika* of Bhāskara.
and c. The *Commentary* called *Vimarshinī* by Kṣhemarāja.

Of these, the *Vārttika* is admittedly of a later date, perhaps of the 11th. century,[3] while what is now known as the *Shiva-Sūtra Vṛitti* is of uncertain authorship. Almost every word of this *Vṛitti* is to be found interspersed in the *Vimarshinī* of Kṣhemarāja. The *Vṛitti* may thus be either an extract from the *Vimarshinī* or it may be an earlier work which was incorporated by Kṣhemarāja in his commentary. This is, however, a point which I have at present no means of deciding.

There are also commentaries on some of the Tantras. Of these the chief ones are the following:—

the *Uddyota*	on the	*Svachchhanda*
do	do	*Netra*
do	do	*Vijñāna-Bhairava*
Vṛitti	do	*Mataṅga*

These commentaries are great attempts to show how the pre-Shiva-Sūtra Tantras taught the Advaita Tattva, although in reality they seem to have taught but plain and unvarnished dualism and even pluralism, like what is described as the Shaiva Darshana in Mādhava's *Sarva Darshana Saṅgraha.* That some of the Tantras had had dualistic interpretations can be definitely proved. We

1. *Vārttika*, सूत्रमाह महेश्वरः or शिवः सूत्रमरीरचत् ।
2. Below p. 23.
3. Below p. 37.

find, for instance, at the end of the Commentary on the *Svachchhanda*, called the *Uddyota*, by Kṣhemarāja, the following verses :—

नाद्यैव भेददृष्टिर्विधुता येनास्वतन्त्रतातत्त्वा ।
श्रीमत्स्वतन्त्रतन्त्रं भेदव्याख्यां न तत् सहते ॥
भेददर्शनसंस्कार-रससंतति-मादितः ।
स्वच्छस्वच्छन्दचित्स्वात्मसतत्त्वं नेक्षते जनः ॥
गतानुगतिकप्रोक्तभेदव्याख्यातमोऽपनुत् ।
तेनाद्वैतामृतस्फीतः स्वच्छन्दोद्द्योत उम्भितः ॥

From this it is clear that the doctrines of the Tantra had previously been understood to represent a dualistic system of philosophy and that it was only after the rise of the Advaita Shaivaism that the Tantra-Shāstra was incorporated into the literature of the Trika by giving a different interpretation to it.[1]

Even the *Mālinī Vijaya*, which is regarded as one of the best authorities[2] on Advaita Shaivaism, containing the true doctrine of the Siddha Yogīshvara, would seem originally to have been a work on dualistic Shaivaism.[3]

---

1. The priority of the Tantras, at least of some of them, may be gathered from allusions to them by Somānanda, for instance, in his reference to the *Mataṅga* and *Svāyambhuva Tantras* and their *Ṭīkās* (*Shiva Dṛiṣhṭi*, iii. 13–15).

2. ....तत्सारं मालिनीमतम्; *Tantrāl. Viv.*, i. p. 34; also *Māl. Vij.*, i. 13.

3. As a prominent example of the adaptation of an older work to suit one's own purpose may be mentioned the *Paramārtha-Sāra* of Abhinava Gupta. It is admittedly based on an older treatise known as the *Ādhāra-Kārikās*. Indeed, the *Paramārtha-Sāra* of Abhinava Gupta is only the *Ādhāra Kārikās* with a few alterations here and there in wording and with the addition of a few verses which are Abhinava Gupta's own and the omission of a few others of the original.

Abhinava Gupta is quite frank about it. For at the very beginning of his task he plainly says that he is going to explain the essence of the Ādhāra Kārikās *according to* (or *in the light of*) *the Shaiva Philosophic system*, शिवदृष्टिशासनयोगेन, which is the same as शिव-(or शैव-) दर्शनशास्त्रयोगेन.

That शिवदृष्टि is the same as शिव-or शैव-दर्शन, or that it may even be the particular treatise called the शिवदृष्टि (or शिवदृष्टिशास्त्र *Parā Triṁ. Viv.* fol. 124 क), which was the first work on the subject, will be shown presently; for दृष्टि meaning दर्शन *i. e.* Philosophy, see p. 18, note 1 below.

That शासन and शास्त्र are interchangeable terms may be gathered from the following use of the words :—

क्रमपूजनमात्रं च कुलपर्वपवित्रकैः ।
सहात्र पूजनं प्रोक्तं सम्यक्त्वं **त्रिकशासने** ॥

यथोक्तम्

द्रवा(व्या ?)णामिव शारीरं वर्णानां सृष्टिबीजकम् ।
शासनानां त्रिकं **शास्त्रं** मोक्षाणां भैरवी स्थितिः ॥

Parā. Triṁ. Viv., fol. 199 क.

The very opening sentence of the commentary on the *Paramārtha-sāra* itself also begins with the words इह शिवाद्वय-**शासने** which, as is obvious, means इह शिवाद्वय- (or शिवाद्वैत-) **शास्त्रे**.

As another instance of the use of शासन meaning a system, or a system of philosophy, see the verse quoted in note 2, p. 2 above and the explanation of शिवशासन occurring in it.

In this connection it may be pointed out that Dr. Barnett in translating this phrase शिवदृष्टिशासनयोगेन by "in mystic vision of Shiva's law" (*J. R. A. S.* for July 1910, p. 719) has, I fear, made a mistake. The commentator, Yogarāja (as he is known in Kashmir and not *Yogamuni*)—whom Abhinava Gupta himself evidently taught for a time (see below p. 35) and who, therefore, must have known his master's meaning—clearly explains the phrase by परमाद्वयस्वस्वरूपस्वातन्त्र्यदृष्ट्या *i. e.* 'according to the view (or philosophy) [which establishes] the Svātantrya of the Svasvarūpa which is Paramādvaya'. The terms left untranslated here are all technical terms which are special to the Shaiva Philosophy of Kashmir; and they clearly show that what the commentator means is that Abhinava Gupta is going to present the original *Ādhāra Kārikās*, or their purport, *in the light of the special doctrines of the Advaita Shaiva Philosophy* or the Trika

Shāstra of Kashmir, the original Kārikās having been written from the standpoint of the Sāṅkhya philosophy—सांख्यनयोक्तोपदेशानुसारेण 'प्रकृतिपुरुषविवेकज्ञानात् परब्रह्मावाप्तिः' इत्येवम्. *Comm.* on *Paramā. Sār.* 3. The contrasting of सांख्यनय, which cannot mean anything but the Sāṅkhya system of philosophy, with शिवदृष्टिशासन would also show that the latter expression means only शिव-(or शैव-) दर्शनशास्त्र, which is a rational system, and not any 'mystic vision,' which must be supra rational, 'of Shiva's law.'

It may also be noted in this connection that Dr. Barnett has most likely been misled in making the following remarks:—

"Our Paramārthasāra must be distinguished from another little work of the same name, of which an edition was published in 1907 at Madras, with a Telugu paraphrase by Paṭṭisapu Veṅkaṭeshvaruḍu. The latter consists of seventy-nine *Āryā* verses; a considerable number of these are borrowed directly from our Paramārthasāra, and with them have been incorporated others, the whole work being painted over with Vaiṣhṇava colours. Needless to say, it is valueless for the criticism of our book." (*J. R. A. S.* 1910, p. 708).

The Madras edition of the work alluded to by Dr. Barnett has not been accessible to me. But I take it to be the same as the one printed originally in the *Shabda-Kalpa-druma*, sub voce वेदान्त, and afterwards republished by Bhuvan Chandra Vasak (Calcutta 1890 A. C.) under the same name. If so, this work is the very *Ādhāra Kārikās* which Abhinava Gupta has admittedly adapted into his *Paramārtha-Sāra*.

MSS. of the *Ādhāra Kārikās*—still known by this very title and not as *Paramārtha-Sāra* as the Calcutta, and presumably also the Madras text, is called—are procurable in Kashmir and I myself possess a copy. They contain practically the same text as the Calcutta (or the Madras) edition. This being the case, the text published in Calcutta (and Madras) is not perhaps so valueless for the criticism of the *Paramārtha-Sāra* of Abhinava Gupta as Dr. Barnett would think. On the contrary, a comparison of the two texts would prove, to my mind, interesting, and I propose to make it on another occasion.

The priority of the text which is published in Calcutta (and Madras) and which is the same text as is still known in Kashmir by the name of *Ādhāra Kārikās i. e.* the Kārikās of Ādhāra or Sheṣhanāga, according to the traditional Kashmiri interpretation (which is justified by the colophon of the Calcutta text), and not as *Paramārtha-Sāra* as said above, can also be proved, I think, by the fact that the verse

सर्वाकारो भगवानुपास्यते येन येन भावेन ।
तं तं भावं भूत्वा चिन्तामणिरिव समभ्येति ॥

quoted in his *Spanda Pradīpikā* (Introduction) by Utpala Vaiṣhṇava (not the famous author of the *Pratyabhijñā Kārikās*), who must have lived earlier than Abhinava Gupta, is not to be found in the latter's *Paramārtha-Sāra* while it occurs both in the Calcutta text as well as in the Kashmir MSS. of the *Ādhāra Kārikās.* My reason for saying that Utpala Vaiṣhṇava lived earlier than Abhinava Gupta and thereby claiming priority in age for the text quoted by him is, in the first place, a local Kashmiri tradition which places him before Abhinava Gupta. Secondly, while we know something, more or less, of almost all writers on Kashmir Shaivaism who flourished *after* Abhinava Gupta and *all* of whom show clear evidence of the influence of this great author, there is no trace whatever in the existing writings of Utpala Vaiṣhṇava either of this influence or of any allusion to Abhinava Gupta. This would be very strange as Utpala seems to have been a profound scholar and quotes from numerous works. Such a writer, if he had lived later than Abhinava Gupta, could not have omitted to quote or allude to the one all dominant and supreme authority on Shaivaism as Abhinava has been considered ever since he flourished in the 11th and 12th centuries of the Christian era.

Moreover, what is now known as the *Ādhāra Kārikās* in Kashmir must have been given that name *after* Abhinava Gupta composed his verses, which he not only adapted from the original Kārikās attributed to Sheṣhanāga, but to which he gave even the very name of the original work. That the original work was known in Kashmir *also* as *Paramā. tha-Sāra* and not as *Ādhāra Kārikās,* prior to Abhinava's treatise, would seem to be established from the fact that these original verses are still known *outside* Kashmir by their ancient name of *Paramārtha-Sāra* and not, as now in Kashmir, *Ādhāra Kārikās,* which name, as just stated, was given to the verses later, to distinguish them from Abhinava's work because this also came to be known as *Paramārtha-Sāra.* If this be so, a Kashmiri author, who in quoting from a text alludes to it, *as Utpala Vaiṣhṇava definitely does,* not by its later Kashmiri designation of *Ādhāra Kārikās* but by its ancient and pre-Abhinava-Guptan name, *Paramārtha-Sāra*, must have lived earlier than Abhinava.

A work, therefore, which is quoted by so ancient and learned an author and authority on Kashmir Shaivaism as Utpala Vaiṣhṇava must be regarded to be, cannot, I fear, be so summarily dismissed as Dr. Barnett is inclined to do.

Finally, because the work in question is, as Dr. Barnett puts it, 'painted over with Vaiṣhṇava colours,' it need not necessarily for that reason be treated with contempt as Dr. Barnett would seem to have done. On the contrary, it would seem to furnish much food for thought—provided my theory as to the age of the text be correct—to a student of the Hindu systems of Philosophy. For it is written—as is evident from even its opening verses and as is admitted explicitly by the commentator on Abhinava's *Paramārtha-Sāra*—from the Sāṅkhya point of view, *i.e.* it is a Sāṅkhya treatise. It is, however, not the form of Sāṅkhya which has been sometimes termed Nirīshvara but rather the other form, the Vaiṣhṇava form—as it may be called, taking the suggestion from Dr. Barnett—which underlies the philosophy of some of the *Purāṇās* and of the *Manu-Saṁhitā* and is to be found treated in the *Mahābhārata*. And if a work on this type of the Sāṅkhya was made the basis of an important treatise by Abhinava, that work itself must have been regarded as very important in those days, so much so that even Abhinava thought it necessary that the then powerful system of Shaivaism should be presented, evidently to command influence, in a similar form. From this fact we may also surmise the place which the Vaiṣhṇava form of the Sāṅkhya must have held in the thought of the country. It would indicate, too, that the Nirīshvara Sāṅkhya, of which the principal authoritative statement must be found in the so-called very recent *Sāṅkhya Sūtras* (and particularly in the much misunderstood Sūtra, ईश्वरासिद्धेः i. 92), is only a later growth, especially as there is hardly a passage which can be construed as an undoubted allusion to the Nirīshvara view, in the older texts either of Īshvara Kṛiṣhṇa or of the *Tattva Samāsa* (also called the *Sāṅkhya Sūtras*). From all these considerations which I hope to develop on another occasion, the text published in Calcutta and Madras as the *Paramārtha-Sāra* and now known in Kashmir as the *Ādhāra Kārikās* becomes an interesting study.

B. THE SPANDA SHĀSTRA—This lays down the main principles of the system in greater detail and in a more amplified form than the *Shiva Sūtras*, without, or hardly, entering into philosophical reasonings in their support.

Of the treatises belonging to this Shāstra, the first and foremost are:—

i. The *Spanda Sūtras*, generally called the *Spanda Kārikās*.

These Sūtras (really verses, numbering 52)[1] are based on the *Shiva Sūtras*, on which they form a sort of running commentary; but a commentary which only enunciates the principles, no doubt in fuller detail, still without entering much into philosophical reasoning. The collection of the *Spanda Sūtras*, is spoken of as a संग्रहग्रन्थ[2] *i. e.* a work which gathers together the meaning of the *Shiva Sūtras*.

The *Spanda Sūtras* are attributed by Kṣhemarāja to Vasugupta himself but they were composed most likely by the latter's pupil, Kallaṭa.

On these *Sūtras* there is,

ii. *The Vṛitti* by Kallaṭa.

The *Vṛitti*, together with the *Sūtras* or *Kārikās*, is called the *Spanda-Sarvasva*.

These are practically all of what now remains of the original Spanda Shāstra.

But on the *Spanda Sūtras* there are the following commentaries:—

---

1. As another example of verses being called Sūtras, the *Pratyabhijñā Sūtras*, which are really verses, may be mentioned.

2. The author of the *Spanda Sūtras* is referred to as संग्रहग्रन्थकृत्; see *Spanda Pradīpikā* on Sūtra 1.

i. The *Vivṛiti* by Rāmakaṇṭha,[1] a pupil of the great Utpala, the son of Udayākara and author of the *Pratyabhijñā-Kārikās.*

ii. The *Pradīpikā* by Utpala—not the same as Utpala, the son of Udayākara, mentioned above. The author of the *Pradīpikā* is traditionally known as Utpala Vaiṣhṇava to distinguish him from his great namesake. Utpala Vaiṣhaṇva lived later than Utpala author of the *Pratyabhijñā* but earlier than Abhinava Gupta.[2]

iii. The *Spanda Sandoha* by Kṣhemarāja. It is a commentary on only the first Sūtra or Kārikā, but explains the purport of the whole work.

iv. *Spanda Nirṇaya,* also by Kṣhemarāja. Of this work only the first section, called the first Niḥṣhyanda, is

---

1. Rāmakaṇṭha was most likely a pupil of Utpala, author of the *Pratyabhijñā,* generally called Utpaladeva or Utpalāchārya, and not of Utpala Vaiṣhṇava, author of the *Spanda Pradīpikā,* who was undoubtedly later than Utpaladeva whom he quotes. He would seem to have lived somewhat later than our Rāmakaṇṭha also. For Utpala Viaṣhṇava quotes Ānandavardhana, author of the *Dhvanyāloka.* Now Ānandavardhana was a contemporary of Muktākaṇa (*Rāj. Tar.*, v. 34) who was an elder brother of Rāmakaṇṭha and therefore must have lived also about the same time as the latter. And if Utpala Vaiṣhṇava lived after Ānandavardhana and therefore after the latter's contemporary, Muktākaṇa, as he undoubtedly did, he must have been also later than Rāmakaṇṭha who was Muktākaṇa's brother.

2. See above note 1; also p. 13. Utpala Vaiṣhṇava was the son of Trivikrama and was born at Nārāyaṇasthāna which is represented by either the modern Nārastān in the Trāl valley, where there still exists an old temple, or the existing village of Narayanthal below Barāmula (most likely the former).

available in Kashmir—at least I have not as yet succeeded in securing a complete MS. of it.[1]

C. THE PRATYABHIJÑĀ SHĀSTRA—This may be regarded as the *manana-* or *vichāra*-Shāstra, *i. e. philosophy proper*,[2] of the Trika. It deals rationally with the doctrines, tries to support them by reasoning and refutes the views of opponents. Indeed, the method of the founder of this Shāstra, the Siddha Somānanda, most probably a pupil of Vasugupata, is said to have been 'the exhaustive treatment of the doctrines of his own system as well as of those of opponents'.[3] Somānanda is also spoken of as the originator of reasoning (**तर्कस्य कर्ता**),[4] namely, in support of the Trika.

The first work which laid the foundation of this branch was

i the *Shiva Dṛiṣhṭi*

by Somānanda himself. As the name implies, *Shiva*

---

1. Dr. Bühler's MS. of the work is entered in his list as a complete one. I have not seen it. But to judge from the number of leaves of which the MS. is said to consist I am very doubtful if it extends beyond the first Niḥṣhyanda.

2. See *Hindu Realism* on Hindu conception of philosophy.

3. तेषां (सोमानन्दपादानां) हि ईदृशी शैली

स्वपक्षान् परपक्षांश्च निःशेषेण न वेद यः ।
स मवयं संशयाम्भोधौ निमज्जंस्तारयेत्कथम् ॥

Parā. Trm̐. Viv. fol. 71. क.

4. '............तर्को योगाङ्गमुत्तमम् ।'

इत्याद्युक्त्या परमोपादेय-स्वप्रकाश स्वात्मेश्वरप्रत्यभिज्ञानपरस्य **तर्कस्य कर्तारो** व्याख्यातारश्च परं नमस्कर्तव्या इति.....................आह

श्रीसोमानन्दबोधश्रीमदुत्पलविनिःसृताः ।
जयन्ति संविदामोदसंदर्भा दिक्प्रसारिणः ॥

Tantrāl. i. 10. with introductory *Viv.*

Here Somānanda is spoken of as तर्कस्य कर्ता (*viz.* in regard to स्वात्मेश्वरप्रत्यभिज्ञा) and Utpala as its व्याख्याता as we positively know the latter was. Needless to say the plural use of कर्तृ and व्याख्यातृ only implies गौरव ।

Drishti, which is the same as *Shiva Darshana*,[1] was *par excellence* the philosophy of Kashmir Shaivaism. Unfortunately the work is not to be had now in its completeness—at least I have not succeeded yet in securing a complete MS. of it nor have I heard of its existence anywhere in Kashmir. So far I have seen only the first-four Āhnikas of the work (the fourth in fragments). But it must have been of a considerable size and must have extended at least to seven Āhnikas, if not more.[2]

Somānanda composed a *Vritti* of his own on the *Shiva Drishti*. But this, with other works of his, are lost now and we know them only by name and from quotations from them.

---

1. The technical term दर्शन, now meaning a system of Philosophy, no doubt originally meant a '*View*' of things,—'a certain way of *looking at* things in general'—and in this sense was certainly interchangeable with the word दृष्टि. The Kashmir authors would seem to have a preference for this latter term which they often used in the technical sense of दर्शन. They were, in this regard, quite like the Buddhist writers who most often used दृष्टि (or its Pāli form दिट्ठि) when they meant दर्शन. But even in the Buddhist literature, as in Kashmiri authors, the use of the word दर्शन (or its equivalent Pāli दस्सन) is not unknown. We find it in its Pāli form, among others, in the *Sāleyyaka Sutta* of the *Majjhima-Nikāya* (*Maj. Ni.* I. v. 1.) and, in its Sanskrit form, in such works as the *Tantrāloka Viveka* (पारमेश्वरे दर्शने; see note 2, p. 2 above) and Utpala's commentary on the *Shiva Drishti*, Āhn. iii. 9.

In Kashmir the word दृक् also would seem to have been used for दर्शन, meaning Philosophy, *i. e.* a certain reasoned '*view*' of things, as, for instance, in the passage:—एषा हि न सांख्यीया न वैदान्तिकी दृक्; *Parā. Trim. Viv.*, fol. 125.

2. A verse quoted in *Parā Trim. Viv.* (fol. 124) is said to be taken from the 7th Āhnika of the *Shiva Drishti*.

The next and now the most important existing work of this Shāstra is

ii the *Īshvara Pratyabhijñā*

or simply the *Pratyabhijñā Sūtras* by Utpala,[1] the famous pupil of Somānanda. It is a work in verses which are called Sūtras.

It is a shorter work than the *Shiva Dṛishṭi* which even in its existing parts contains more than 307 anushṭubh verses, while the total number, of verses in the *Pratyabhijña Sūtras* is only 190.[2]

In his own Sūtras or verses, Utpala summarised the teaching of his master Somānanda. Indeed, his *Īshvara Pratyabhijñā* is spoken of as only "the reflection of the wisdom taught by Somānanda."[3]

Being a shorter and more compact work the *Pratyabhijñā* would seem to have superseded, to a great extent at least, the *Shiva Dṛishṭi* of Somānanda. Indeed, the *Pratyabhijñā* assumed such an important position

---

1. This Utpala was, as said above, other than the author of the *Spanda Paradīpikā*.

2. *Viz.*:—

88 verses in the First Adhikāra (subdivided into 4 Āhnikas)
53 verses in the Second Adhikāra (subdivided likewise into 4 Āhnikas)
31 do in the Third Adhikāra (subdivided into 2 Āhnikas)
and 18 do in the Fourth Adhikāra (making only one Āhnika)

There is a discrepancy in the numbering of the verses in different Mss. leading at first to the notion that the total numbers in them really vary. But this is not the case. They all contain the same number of verses which for each Āhnika has been fixed by the Commentary.

3. श्रीसोमानन्दनाथस्य विज्ञानप्रतिबिम्बकम् ।

Īshv. Pra Vim., Intro.verse 2.

that the whole system of the Shaiva Philosophy of Kashmir would seem to have come to be known, outside Kashmir, as the *Pratyabhijñā Darshana*, under which name Mādhavāchārya treats of the Trika in his *Sarva Darshana Saṅgraha.*[1]

However this may be, round the *Sūtras* or *Kārikās* of Utpala there grew up a mass of literature; and the *Pratyabhijñā Sūtras*, together with the various Commentaries on them and with other works which drew their inspiration from the *Sūtras*, now constitute perhaps the greater portion of the existing writings on Kashmir Shaivaism.

Of the commentaries on the *Pratyabhijñā Sūtras*, the following are still available, either complete or in parts:—

a. The *Vṛitti* by Utpala himself (available only incomplete—up to verse 161 *i. e.* III. ii. 9.)[2]

a. The *Pratyabhijñā Vimarshinī* by Abhinava Gupta (complete), also called the *Laghvī Vṛitti i. e.* the Shorter Commentary.

c. The *Pratyabhijñā Vivṛiti Vimarshinī*, also called the *Bṛihatī Vṛitti* or Longer Commentary, by the same author.

1. What Mādhavāchārya describes as *Shaiva Darshana* is, as a dualistic system, fundamentally different from the monistic Philosophy which constitutes Kashmir Shaivaism. See below Part II; also *Bhandarkar*, p. 81.

2. Utpala wrote also a *Ṭīkā* on his *Vṛitti*. It must have been called '*Vivṛiti*' and is practically lost now. I have seen only a few leaves of a mutilated Ms. of the work. For the rest, we are left to infer what it must have been like from the pratīkas quoted in the *Pratyabhijñā-Vivṛiti-Vimarshinī* (or the *Bṛihatī Vṛitti* as it is also called) of Abhinava Gupta.

Utpala also wrote a commentary on his Master's *Shiva Dṛishṭi*, but it can now be had, like the latter work, only in fragments.

This latter work is a Commentary really on the lost Ṭīkā, presumably called the Vivṛiti, on the Sūtras by Utpala himself.Complete MSS. of this work are very rare in Kashmir. I have seen only one complete MS. of the work and have heard of the existence of only one other.[1]

In addition to these three main divisions of the Shaiva literature there are also

(*a*) a number of compositions called "Stotras," which give expression to the Philosophical doctrines of the system in a devotional form and occupy the same position in this system as the Vedānta Stotras do in the Vedānta system; and

(*b*) a number of compositions on the daily practices and ceremonials to be performed by a Shaiva.

These two classes, however, may be regarded as forming parts of the three main groups named above—class (*a*) belonging to the groups B and C, and (*b*) to A.

Finally there is the great work, *Tantrāloka*, by Abhinava Gupta, which forms a class by itself and deals comprehensively with Shaivaism in all its aspects.[2]

---

1. The MS. (in Devanāgarī characters) of this work purchased for the Government by Dr. Bühler (No. 464 in his list) is also complete.

2. *a*. MSS. of this work, so far as the text alone is concerned, are plentiful. It had a commentary also, called *Viveka;* but of this work complete MSS. are very rare,—I might say, not available. All MSS. of the work that I have seen end at the 10th chapter. Dr. Bühler's MS. of the *Viveka* which he procured at Delhi, is entered in his list as complete; but I doubt it very much. For what is given as an extract from the beginning of this MS. (See *Report* pp. xxix and cxlviii) is really the beginning of the *Parā Trimshikā Vivaraṇa* of Abhinava Gupta and not of the *Viveka* at all.

b. In addition to the works mentioned above, the *Paramārtha-Sāra* of Abhinava Gupta with its *Commentary*

Of these three branches of the Kashmir Shaiva literature the first, that is the Āgama Shāstra, is attributed to Shiva himself who is represented in the Tantra section of this Shāstra as explaining the doctrines and practices of Shaivaism, generally to Pārvatī in answer to her questions, while He is believed to have Himself composed the *Shiva Sūtras*, in which He laid down the principles in a compact form and which were revealed to Vasugupta; the second was originated either by Vasugupta himself or by his pupil Kallaṭa; while the third was founded by Siddha Somānanda.

Leaving aside the Āgama Shāstra, including the *Shiva Sūtras* of which the authorship is attributed to

---

by his pupil Yogarāja and the *Pratyabhijñā-Hṛidaya* of Kṣhemarāja may be mentioned as important works on the system. For the true character of the *Paramārtha-Sāra*, see *ante* p. 10, note 3. *PratyabhijñāHṛidaya* is a small compendium and may be said to bear, more or less, the same relation to the system as the Vedānta-Sāra of Sadānanda bears to the Vedānta system.

Both these works are included in this series (the Kashmir Series of Texts and Studies).

c. The classification given above of the main branches of Shaiva literature of Kashmir is not what would be regarded as orthodox. The followers of the system no doubt recognise a three-fold classification but on a different principle. According to this method the three classes of the literature are called

(a) Parā (Higher),

(b) Aparā (Lower)

and (c) Parāparā (Higher-lower *i. e.* all-inclusive).

What deals with the purely doctrinal aspect of the subject, either as a system of Faith or Philosophy (ज्ञानप्रधान), such as the *Shiva Dṛiṣhṭi*, is termed Parā, while the branch dealing chiefly with the practical and ritual part (क्रियाप्रधान), like the *Svachchhanda Tantra*, is called Aparā. The Parāparā combines in it the nature of both, and is therefore regarded as superior to either.

Shiva Himself, we have to regard Vasugupta and Somānanda as the human founders of the Advaita Shaivaism which is peculiar to Kashmir.

Of these two again, while Vasugupta gave out the doctrines merely as revelations and articles of faith, Somānanda, who was most likely a pupil of Vasugupta,[1] laid the the foundation of their philosophy.

Of the personality and lineage of Vasugupta we know little from himself. If he recorded anything on these points, it is lost with most of his writings. Whatever little we know now of him is from his pupils, who tell us that he lived in retirement, as a holy sage, in the charming valley of what is now called the Hārwan stream (the ancient Ṣhaḍarhad-vana) behind the Shālimār garden near Srinagar.[2]

And we can also gather from the *Rāja Taraṅgiṇī*, v. 66, which states that Kallaṭa flourished in the reign of king Avanti-Varman of Kashmir *i. e.* in the latter half of the 9th Christian century, that Vasugupta, Kallaṭa's Guru, must have taught not much earlier than the first half of the same century, *i. e.*, either at the end of the 8th or the beginning of the 9th century A. C.

While we know nothing more than this about Vasugupta, Somānanda, the founder of the Pratyabhijñā Shāstra tells us a good deal about his lineage. We find the following account given by Somānanda himself:—

शैवादीनि रहस्यानि पूर्वमासन्महात्मनाम् ।
ऋषीणां वक्त्रकुहरे तेष्वेवानुग्रहक्रिया ॥
कलौ प्रवृत्ते यातेषु तेषु दुर्गमगोचरम् ।
कलापिग्रामप्रमुखमुच्छिन्ने शिवशासने ॥
कैलासाद्रौ भ्रमन्देवो मूर्त्या श्रीकण्ठरूपया ।
अनुग्रहायावतीर्णश्चोदयामास भूतले ॥
मुनिं दुर्वाससं नाम भगवानूर्ध्वरेतसम् ।
नोच्छिद्यते यथा शास्त्रं रहस्यं कुरु तादृशम् ॥

---

1. See below p. 25.

2. See illustration No. 1 (of the Mahādevagiri and its valley) in the Shiva Sūtra Vimarshinī (vol. I of this series).

ततः स भगवान्देवादादेशं प्राप्य यत्नवान् ।
ससर्ज मानसं पुत्रं त्र्यम्बकादित्यनामकम् ॥
तस्मिन् संक्रामयामास रहस्यानि समन्ततः ।
सोऽपि गत्वा गुहां सम्यक् त्र्यम्बकाख्यस्ततः परम् ॥
ज्ञानमभ्यासकाष्ठां तन्नीतवान् स गुहान्तरे ।
तन्नाम्ना चिह्निता सापि गुहा ख्यातात्र भूतले ॥
स तत्र ज्ञानसंसिद्ध्या ससर्ज मनसा सुतम् ।
खस्योत्पतनसंसिद्धस्तत्पुत्रोऽपि यथा तथा ॥
सिद्धस्तद्वत्सुतोत्पत्त्या सिद्धा एवं चतुर्दश ।
यावत्पञ्चदशः पुत्रः सर्वशास्त्रविशारदः ॥
स कदाचिद्रागवशात् कुतश्चिद्ब्राह्मणात् स्वयम् ।
ब्राह्मणीमानयामास ततो जातस्तथाविधः ॥
तनयः स च कालेन कश्मीरेष्वागतो भ्रमन् ।
नाम्ना स संङ्गमादित्यो वर्षादित्यस्तु तत्सुतः ॥
तस्याप्यभूत् स भगवान् अरुणादित्यसंज्ञकः ।
आनन्दसंज्ञकस्तस्मात्स बभूव तथाविधः ॥
तस्मादस्मि समुद्भूतः सोमानन्दाख्य ईदृशः ॥[1]

---

1. The above passage is found quoted in certain MSS. where it is introduced with the words—तदुक्तं शिवदृष्टिवृत्तौ. From this it is clear that it originally occurred in the now lost *Vṛitti* composed by Somānanda himself on his own great work *Shiva Dṛishṭi.*

We learn from this extract that Somānanda claimed to be descended from the sage Durvāsas,—who had been commanded by Shiva as Shrīkaṇṭha to teach anew the Shivāgama,—through the line of that sage's 'mind born' son Tryambaka whom Durvāsas appointed to spread the knowlege of the Trika aspect of the Shivāgama as we are told in the Tantrāloka (above p. 6 with note 1). Up to the 15th generation the race of Tryambaka was continued by sons who had all been produced by their respective parents by the power of the mind, *i. e.* they were all born not of woman's womb but of the mind and were thus 'mind born sons.' The representative, however, of the 15th generation violated this rule and being enamoured of the daughter of a certain Brahmin took her for a wife and had born of her a son. This son, who was named Saṅgamāditya, the first in the line to be born of a woman's womb, came, in the course of his wanderings, to Kashmir where he settled. Of him there was born Varṣhāditya who had a son named Aruṇāditya. Aruṇāditya had a son, Ānanda by name. It is of this Ānanda that Somānanda was born.

While thus we know something of Somānanda's descent in his own words, we know the period when he must have lived from that of the great scholar and Shaiva teacher, Mahāmāheshvara Abhinava Gupta, who lived, as we know from his own statements, towards the end of the tenth and the first quarter of the 11th Christian century and who was the fourth in succession from Somananda in a line of spiritual discipleship. Somānanda was followed by his famous pupil Utpala, son of Udayākara and author of the *Īshvara Pratyabhijñā* Kārikās and many other works; and he by Lakshmaṇa Gupta who was the Guru of Abhinava Gupta. Somānanda thus having flourished four generations ealier than Abhinava Gupta must have lived towards the end of the ninth century,[1] and as said above,[2] was most likely a pupil of Vasugupta[3] who flourished at about the same period or somewhat earlier.

---

1. Bühler's *Report* p. 82.
2. Ante p. 17.
3. In the *Ṭīkā* on the *Shāradā-Tilaka*, the following passage occurs:—

श्रीकण्ठं वसुमन्तं (वसुगुप्तं) सोमानन्दं तथोत्पलाचार्यम् ।
लक्ष्मणमभिनवगुप्तं वन्दे श्रीक्षेमराजं च ॥

Of the names mentioned herein, Somānanda, Utpala Lakṣhmaṇa, Abhinava and Kṣhemarāja form, as we know, a line of spiritual succession *i. e.* गुरुपरम्परा. It is also evident from the context that the passage is intended to record the line of spiritual succession of the Shaiva teachers of Kashmir. This being so, and also in view of the fact that five names out of the seven mentioned in the list *do* represent such a line, it is quite reasonable to conclude that the remaining two also belong to the same line. If this conclusion be right, then Somānanda was undoubtedly a pupil of Vasugupta, who on his own part, had for his Guru Shiva himself as Shrīkaṇṭha, as stated in the Kashmiri tradition found embodied in the following verse

जयति गुरुरेक एव श्रीश्रीकण्ठो भुवि प्रथितः ।
तदपरमूर्तिर्भगवान् महेश्वरो भूतिराजश्च ॥ *Tantrāl.* Āhn. i. 9.

The age of Somānanda also points to the same conclusion, specially as we find nothing antagonistic to Vasugupta's view in the writings of Somānanda who only supports by philosophic reasoning what had been taught by Vasugupta chiefly as matters of faith and religion.

Thus it will be seen that the origin of both the Advaita Shaiva *Faith* and *Philosophy* of Kashmir—as the teachings of the Āgama and Spanda Shāstras on the one hand and of the Pratyabhijñā Shāstra on the other may respectively be called—must be traced to the end of the 8th or the beginning of the 9th century A. C.; and they were then founded by men who were both regarded as holy sages.

One of them, Somānanda, claimed descent from the great sage Durvāsas himself and his "mind-born" son Tryambaka, while about the other, wonderful stories are told. One of these stories is connected with the origin of the *Shiva Sūtras* themselves.

We are told in the *Shiva Sūtra Vimarshinī*, that Vasugupta, while residing in his hermitage below the Mahādeva peak,[1] had one night a dream in which Shiva, who was moved to compassion to see the world immersed in spiritual darkness, appeared and disclosed to the sage the existence of certain Sūtras—embodying the essence of the Shiva Shāsana—which were to be found inscribed on a rock. The rock had been, Vasugupta was informed in the dream, lying in a certain part of the valley, with the inscribed side turned downwards and hidden from the profane gaze. But if he went there in the morning, he was also told in the dream, the rock would turn over of its own accord by his very touch and he should then learn the Sūtras of which the meaning would be revealed to him and he should teach them to worthy pupils. A huge rock represented in the second illustration published in the *Shiva-Sūtra-Vimarshinī* is still pointed out as the one upon which these Sūtras were found inscribed, although no trace whatever of any inscription on it is now to be detected. The rock goes by the name of Shaṅkarpal which may be merely a corrupt form of the

1. See illustration No. 1 in the *Shiva-Sūtra Vimarshinī*. The peak is indicated there by an arrow-mark.

Sanskrit Shaṅkaropala ; and the Sūtras found thereon are, according to Kṣhemarāja, the very ones which were expounded by him in his *Vimarshinī* and which are now printed as a whole, for the first time as far as I know.[1]

There is, however, a different version of this tradition.[2] It has been recorded by at least three writers, Rājānaka

---

1. A portion of the Sūtras together with a translation of a part of the *Vimarshinī* appeared in the *Theosophist* (Madras) for 1908. The author of this translation, labouring far away from Kashmir and ignorant of local tradition, naturally made many mistakes. He did not even know that Mahādeva-Giri meant a particular mountain in the valley of Kashmir and took it for a name of Kailāsa.

2. Perhaps the earliest record of the version of the tradition which states that the Sūtras were imparted to Vasugupta *by Shiva himself in a dream*, is to be found in the *Spanda Vṛitti* by Kallaṭa who says :—

लब्धं महादेवगिरौ महेशस्वप्नोपदिष्टाच्छिवसूत्रसिन्धोः ।
स्पन्दामृतं यद्वसुगुप्तपादैः श्रीकल्लटस्तत् प्रकटीचकार ॥

But it knows nothing of the Sūtras having been found inscribed on a rock as related by Kṣhemarāja, who most likely records a later development of the original tradition which simply stated that Vasugupta got the Sūtras, not in the ordinary way from a mortal Guru, but from Mahādeva himself and in a dream in which Mahādeva appeared to him and taught him the Sūtras.

This would also account for Shiva himself (as Shrīkaṇṭha) having been regarded as the Guru of Vasugupta as stated in the passage quoted above from the *Shāradā-Tilaka-Ṭīkā* and maintained by local tradition.

About the authenticity of the above verse, however, as a composition of Kallaṭa, there is some doubt. For while it is no doubt found at the end of the MSS. of the *Vṛitti* by Kallaṭa, it was evidently regarded, by the scribe of the Manuscript (or its archetype) now in the India Office Library in London and entered in its *Catalogue of Sanskrit*

Rāma or Rāmakaṇṭha,[1] author of the *Spanda Vivṛiti*, Utpala, son of Trivikrama and author of the *Spanda Pradīpikā* and finally by Bhāskara, son of Divākara and author of the *Shiva Sūtra Vārttika*. According to this version the Sūtras, although composed by Shiva himself,[2] were taught to Vasugupta by a Siddha *i. e.* a

---

MSS. (p. 832), as belonging to the *Vivṛiti* of Rāmakaṇṭha. In Dr. Bhandarkar's MS. also (*Report* p. 77), the verse is similarly treated *i. e.* as belonging to the *Vivṛiti* (or *Vivaraṇa*) of Rāmakaṇṭha.

But if the verse is not a composition of Kallaṭa, it is equally doubtful if it is either by Rāmakaṇṭha to whom it is evidently attributed in the India Office and Bhandarkar MSS. It not only does not occur in the MSS. of the *Vivṛiti* I have seen but Rāmakaṇṭha could not have written it without contradicting himself. For while in this verse, he would be saying,—if he were really its author—that Vasugupta was taught the *Shiva Sūtras* by Mahādeva in a dream, he has said just a few lines above, in explaining the 52nd Kārikā (अगाधसंशयाम्भोधि &c.) that his master received these very things—for the words समस्तरहस्योपतिषद्भूतस्पन्दतत्त्व cannot possibly mean anything else—*not* from Shiva but from a Siddha. Surely he could not contradict himself so soon.

1. This Rāma or Rāmakaṇṭha is said to have been one of the pupils of Utpala, author of the *Pratyabhijñā Sūtras*, and as such a fellow student of Lakṣhmaṇa, Guru of Abhinava Gupta. He therefore either was a contemporary of or lived slightly earlier than Utpala Vaiṣhṇava, son of Trivikrama and author of the *Spanda Pradīpikā*. This Utpala lived as we know later than Utpala, the Pratayabhijñākāra, but must have been senior to Abhinava Gupta as I have tried to show above (p. 10-14, note 3.)

2. See *Vārttika* where the Sūtras are often introduced with such phrases as सूत्रमाह महेश्वरः or शिवः सूत्रमरीरचत्. Comp. also the closing statement of the same work which is

इतिप्रकरणत्रयं सुघटमीषदुन्मीलितं मया शिवमुखोद्गतं सुमतिसिद्धये सांप्रतम् ।
विचार्य गतमत्सरैर्बुधजनैर्गुणग्राहिभिः सुसेव्यमिह तेष्वलं भवतु सिद्धिमोक्षप्रदम् ॥

super-human being with high spiritual attainments. In other words Vasugupta did *not* find them inscribed on a rock—their existence in this form having been revealed to him by Shiva in a dream—as related by Kṣhemarāja. This is most likely the original version of the tradition, unless we regard what is recorded by Kallaṭa, who was a pupil of Vasugupta himself, as the original tradition, which, while not knowing anything of the Sūtras having been found inscribed on a rock, *did* state, as said above, that they were taught by Shiva himself—and *not* by a Siddha—in a dream. Kṣhemarāja is, as far as I know, the only writer who gives the other version. It, however, seems certain that although the original version knew nothing of the Sūtras having been found inscribed on a rock and of Shiva himself having given Vasugupta, in a dream, the information of their existence in this form, it *did* know that either a Siddha or Shiva himself taught the Sūtras to Vasugupta, *not in the ordinary way but in a dream*, and that the Sūtras so taught to Vasugupta were the composition of Shiva himself.

However this may be, and however Vasugupta may have obtained them, it is clear that the *Shiva Sūtras* as taught by him laid the foundation of the Advaita Shivaism of Kashmir—or, of the Trika, as it is called.

It is also clear from all accounts that the chief agent by whom Vasugupta had his teachings promulgated was his pupil Kallaṭa, who lived, according to the *Rāja Taraṅgiṇī*, in the days of king Avanti-Varman (855–883 A. C.), as said above. But there is a difference of opinion as to how this was done. According to the tradition, which is recorded by Kṣhemarāja[1] and which would seem in later times

---

1. See his Introductions to the *Spanda Sandoha* and the *Spanda Nirṇaya* and also *Shiv. Sū. Vim.* पृ० २.

to have been generally accepted[1] in Kashmir, Vasugupta himself wrote the *Spanda Sūtras* or *Kārikās* basing them on the *Shiva Sūtras*, which had been revealed to him. And the *Spanda Sūtras* thus composed by himself were taught by him, along with the *Shiva Sūtras*, to Kallaṭa and other pupils, while Kallaṭa spread their knowledge by writing commentaries on them.

But what seems to be the older, and perhaps correct, account is given, among others, by Rāma, author of the *Spanda Vivṛiti*, Utpala Vaishṇava[2] and Bhāskara, author of the *Shiva Sūtra Vārttika*. The last named of the three, Bhāskara, gives the tradition in some detail. He says:—

"Formerly, on the holy Mahādeva mountain, the *Shiva Sūtras* with their mysterious meanings were

---

1. To judge from the colophons of MSS. of the Kārikās only (without the commentaries) wherein they are always ascribed to Vasugupta.

2. Rāmakaṇṭha explains the phrase गुरुभारती at the end of the *Kārikās* as the words of Vasugupta thereby evidently meaning that the *Kārikās* were composed by Kallaṭa embodying therein the 'words' of his master.

Utpala Vaishṇava says:—

अयमत्र किलाम्नायः सिद्धमुखेनागतं रहस्यं यत् ।
तद्भट्टकल्लटेन्दुर्वसुगुप्तगुरोरवाप्य शिष्याणाम् ।
अवबोधार्थमनुष्टुप्-पञ्चाशिकयात्र संग्रहं कृतवान् ॥ *Sp. Prad.*, Intro.

He also reads the following at the end as part of the original:—

वसुगुप्तादवाप्येदं गुरोस्तत्त्वार्थदर्शिनः ।
रहस्यं श्लोकयामास सम्यक् श्रीभट्टकल्लटः ॥

This verse, however, is not to be found in the MSS. of the *Spanda Vṛitti* by Kallaṭa or of the *Vivṛiti* by Rāmakaṇṭha.

revealed to the Guru, Vasugupta, by the teachings of a Siddha. He then transmitted them to the revered and learned Kallaṭa Bhaṭṭa. Having received, in this way, these Sūtras in four parts, he afterwards expounded three parts out of the four by his own *Spanda Sūtras* and the last part by the *Ṭīkā* called the *Tattvārtha-Chintāmaṇi*".[1]

---

1. Translated, more or less freely, from the following orginal:—

श्रीमन्महादेवगिरौ वसुगुप्तगुरोः पुरा ।
सिद्धादेशात् प्रादुरासञ्छिवसूत्राणि तस्य हि ॥
सरहस्यान्यतः सोऽपि प्रादाद्भट्टाय सूरये ।
श्रीकल्लटाय सोऽप्येवं चतुःखण्डानि तान्यथ ॥
व्याकरोत्त्रिकमेतेभ्यः स्पन्दसूत्रैः स्वकैस्ततः ।
तत्त्वार्थचिन्तामण्याख्यटीकया खण्डमन्तिमम् ॥

The word त्रिक in the above does not refer, as might be supposed, to the techincal name of the system or to the triple principles of शिव–शक्ति–अणु which that name implies, but to the three divisions out of the four into which the *Shiva Sūtras* would seem to have been divided. Only three divisions of the *Shiva Sūtras*, alluded to here as त्रिक, very likely formed the basis of the *Spanda Sūtras* or *Kārikās*, while the fourth division of the Sūtras were apparently reserved for a different treatment, namely, in the form of a commentary, properly so called, on them. This commentary on the fourth division of the *Shiva Sūtras*, as distinguished from the *Kārikās* written on the other three divisions, was called *Tattvārtha Chintāmaṇi* and is now lost. We now know it only from quotations made from it, as for instance in *the Shiv. Sū. Vim.*, *Parā Triṁ. Viv.*, fol. 62 and *Pratybhijñā Hṛidaya.*

Kallaṭa would seem to have written a Commentary, properly so called, also on the three divisions of the *Shiva Sūtras* which apparently formed the basis of the *Spanda Kārikās*. It seems to have been called *Madhuvāhinī*, to judge from the following passage occuring in the *Prat. Viv. Vim.* (Bṛihatī):—

तदुक्तमिति शिवसूत्रवृत्त्योर्मधुवाहिनीतत्त्वार्थचिन्तामण्योर्भट्टश्रीकल्लटपादैः ।

From the above it would appear that Vasugupta did no more than simply transmit the Sūtras with their meanings to Kallaṭa who spread their knowledge by writing explanatory treatises on them, one of these treatises being called the *Spanda Sūtras,* which are no other than what are now generally called the *Spanda Kārikās.*[1] It is however possible that Vasugupta wrote a work called *Spandāmṛita,*[2] which Kallaṭa made use of in composing his *Spanda Sūtras* or *Kārikās.* Indeed his *Spanda Sūtras* may not be anything more than the *Spandāmṛita* of Vasugupta with only a few additions and alterations of his own,[3] very much like the *Paramārtha-*

As the commentary *Tattvāratha Chintāmaṇi* is expressly said to have been written on the fourth division of the *Shiva Sūtras*, this other commentary, *Madhuvāhinī,* was composed very likely on the three divisions of the *Shiva Sūtras* which formed the basis of the *Spanda Kārikās.*

The statement that the *Spanda Kārikās* were based only on three, out of the four, divisions of the *Shiva Sūtras* would seem to be justified by the fact that Kallaṭa's own *Vṛitti* on the *Spanda Kārikās* divides the latter work also into three sections (not four as in the *Vivṛiti* of Rāmakanṭha who was a later writer).

1. That the *Spanda Kārikās* and the *Spanda Sūtras* are the same may be gathered from *Shiv. Sū. Vim.*, पृ० १ and also from references made explicitly to the *Kārikās* as *Sūtras,* for instance, by Rāmakanṭha speaking of them as स्पन्दार्थसूत्रावली.

2. See the verse quoted in note 2, p. 27 above.

3. This theory, if accepted, has the advantage that it would account for the phrase गुरुभारती in the 52nd Kārikā referred to above (p. 30). It would also explain why the divisions of the *Kārikās* according to Kallaṭa's own *Vṛitti* are called Niḥṣhyandas or streams, namely, of the 'amṛita of Spanda.' And if Kallaṭa retained even the name given to the sections of the original, it is not likely that he altered much of the original composition of his master.

Sāra of the great Abhinava Gupta, who in later times adapted the old *Ādhāra Kārikās* attributed to *Sheṣha Nāga* to something suited to his own purpose.[1] Kallaṭa wrote on the *Spanda Kārikās* also a short *Vṛitti* which, together with the Kārikās, is called *Spanda Sarvasva.* In the *Spanda Sarvasva,* Kallaṭa 'gathered together[2]' the meaning of the *Shiva Sūtras;* while evidently on some of the latter he wrote a commentary, the *Tattavārtha Chintāmaṇi,* and also perhaps another, named the *Madhuvāhinī;*[3] and together with these he handed down the *Shiva Sūtras* to his pupil Pradyumna Bhaṭṭa who was also a cousin of his, being a son of his maternal uncle. Pradyumna Bhaṭṭa in his turn handed the teaching to his son Prajñārjuna and he to his pupil Mahādeva. The latter again transmitted it on to his son Shrīkaṇṭha Bhaṭṭa from whom Bhāskara, son of Divākara, received them and wrote his *Vārttika* on them.[4]

It would also seem to account, on the one hand, for the use of the words श्रीकल्लटस्तत् प्रकटीचकार in the verse quoted in note 2, p. 27 above, and, on the other, for the colophons found in all MSS. which I have seen of the *Spanda Kārikās* by themselves, in which they are invariably attributed to Vasugupta.

1. See above p. 10, note 3.

2. The '*Spanda Kārikās*' are spoken of as a संग्रहग्रन्थ; see above note 2, p. 15; also 'संग्रहं कृतवान्' in *Sp. Prad.* Intro.

3. See note 1, p. 31 above.

4. एवं रहस्यमप्येष मातुलेयाय चावदत् ।
श्रीमत्प्रद्युम्नभट्टाय सोऽपि स्वतनयाय च ॥
श्रीमत्प्रज्ञार्जुनाख्याय प्रादात्सोऽप्येवमावदत् ।
श्रीमहादेवभट्टाय स्वशिष्यायाप्यसौ पुनः ॥
श्रीमच्छ्रीकण्ठभट्टाय प्रददौ स्वसुताय च ।
तस्मात्प्राप्य करोम्येष सूत्रवार्तिकमादरात् ॥
दैवाकरिर्भास्करोऽहमन्तेवासिगणेरितः ।

Continuation of passage quoted in note 1, p. 31. The एष in the first line of this portion of the extract refers of course to Kallaṭa.

In the *Vārttika* of Bhāskara, therefore, we have got what Kallaṭa must have taught as, in all essentials, the meaning of the *Shiva Sūtras*. And we can see at once from it that Kallaṭa handed down the teaching merely as religious doctrines, which he no doubt explained in some detail without, or hardly, entering into any philosophical reasoning in their support.

Yet in a country like India, where philosophic reasoning has from early times played such an important part, it was essential for any system of religion to give full philosophical reasons in its support, if it was at all to hold its own, especially in an age when Buddhism exercised such a great influence as it did in Kashmir about the time the Advaita Shaivaism as represented by the Trika made its appearance. This need must have been felt almost from the beginning—a need which was not met by the writings of Kallaṭa. And it was undoubtedly to meet this necessity that there grew up another line of activity supplementing that followed by Kallaṭa. This was started by the Siddha Somānanda, who like Kallaṭa may have been a pupil of Vasugupta himself.[1] While Kallaṭa may be said to have handed down the doctrines as a system of religion, Somānanda supplied the logical reasoning in their support and made a system of Advaita Philosophy of what was at first taught as a system of faith, and thus founded the Pratyabhijñā Shāstra which is mentioned above and which is so named after the *Pratyabhijñā Sūtras* or *Kārikās* of his pupil Utpala.

And as, for the success of a religion in a philosophic land like India, it was necessary to lay greater stress on the philosophical reason of the religion, the work of Somānanda was carried on in greater detail by Utpala and Abhinava Gupta, his great successors in the line of

---

1. Above note 3, p. 25.

discipleship. This branch, therefore, forms perhaps a far larger portion of the Shaiva literature of Kashmir than either of the other two. Indeed, the Pratyabhijñā method of treating the Shaiva doctrines came to be regarded as so important that it was adopted, more or less, practically by all subsequent writers on the subject. Among these later writers are to be mentioned:

1. Kṣhemarāja, who was the author of the *Shiva Sūtra Vimarshinī* and several other works,[1] and who was a pupil of Abhinava Gupta;

2. Yogarāja, author of the *Commentary* on Abhinava Gupta's *Paramārtha-Sāra-Saṅgraha* and a pupil apparently of both Abhinava Gupta and Kṣhemarāja;[2]

---

1. The *chief* existing works of Kṣhemarāja are:-

Pratyabhijñā Hṛidaya
Spanda Sandoha
Spanda Nirṇaya
Svachchhandoddyota
Netroddyota
Vijñāna-Bhairavoddyota
(only a portion of this work exists incorporated in Shivopādhyāya's commentary on the *Vijñāna Bhairava*. See the concluding verse of the latter work).
Shiva Sūtra Vṛitti (?)
(see *ante* p. 9)
Shiva Sūtra Vimarshinī
Stava Chintāmaṇi Ṭīkā
Utpala-Stotrāvalī Ṭīkā
Parā-Prāveshikā
Tattva Sandoha
&c. &c.

2. See the second of the introductory verses and the last verse of his *Paramārtha-Sāra Vivṛiti.*

3. Jayaratha, commentator on the *Tantrāloka* of Abhinava Gupta; and

4. Shivopādhyāya, author of a *Commentary* on the *Vijñāna Bhairava*.

Kṣhemarāja being a pupil of Abhinava Gupta must have lived and written in the eleventh Christian century and Yogarāja, being junior to Kṣhemarāja, may be considered as having continued the labours of his masters till either the end of the same or the beginning of the 12th century; whereas Jayaratha and Shivopādhyāya must have lived in the 12th[1] and the 18th[2] centuries A. C. respectively. After this date we do not find any great writer on the Shaivaism of Kashmir and the history of its literature may be regarded as closed, although the Shaiva faith is still living in the valley and there are also a few Paṇḍits[3] who still continue the study of its literature at least in some of its branches. The study of most of them, however, does not go beyond the *Spanda-Kārikās* and the *Pratyabhiñjā-Hṛidaya*, a compendium of only 20 Sūtras by Kṣhemarāja.

Such is the end of the Shaivaism of Kashmir and of its history which may be summarised in a tabulated form as follows:—

---

1. Bühler's *Report* pp. 82 and cxlix to cliv.

2. For an account and date of Sukha Jīvana in whose time Shivopādhyāya lived and wrote, see Hasan Shah's *Persian History of Kashmir*.

3. The word *Paṇḍit* as used in Kashmir now unfortunately means any descendant of a Bhahmin family who still keeps within the fold of the Hindu community, no matter how ignorant and illiterate he may be, and there are hundreds, if not thousands, of 'Paṇḍits' who are *absolutely* illiterate.

Shrīkaṇṭha......... Guru of Vasugupta and also, as Shiva, author and promulgator of the *Āgamas* (Tantras) and author of the *Shiva Sūtras.*

|

Vasugupta......... Flourished in the first half of the 9th century A. C. and inspirationally received the *Shiva Sūtras* which laid the foundation of Kashmir Shaivaism or the Trika, as a *system of Religion.*

|

Kallaṭa (pupil of above) spread the teachings of his master chiefly as a religion; lived in the second half of the 9th century A. C.

|

Pradyumna Bhaṭṭa (cousin, *i.e.* mātuleya, and pupil).

|

Prajñārjuna (son and pupil)

|

Mahādeva Bhaṭṭa (pupil).

|

Shrīkaṇṭha Bhaṭṭa (son and pupil).

|

Bhāskara, (pupil of above and son of Divākara); lived probably in the 11th century A. C. and embodied in his *Shiva Sūtra Vārttika* the teachings of Vasugupta received along the above line of spiritual succession.

Somānanda, probably also a pupil of Vasugupta and lived towards the end of the 9th century A. C. Supplied philosophical reasonings in support of his master's teachings and thus laid the foundation of the Advaita Shaivaism, or 'Trika' as a *system of Philosophy.*

|

Utpala or Utpalācharya, pupil of Somānanda; wrote the *Īshvara-Pratyabhijñā Kārikās* or *Sūtras* and embodied therein in a more compact form the teachings of his master.

Lakshmaṇa
(son and pupil).=

Abhinava Gupta, pupil of above. Great Shaiva author; wrote Commentaries on Utpalāchārya's Works, on the *Parā-Triṁshikā* (Tantra) and composed the great work *Tantrāloka* which is an independent treatise&the *Tantrasāra*, besides numerous other works. He thus became the one dominant influence of his own and subsequent ages in all matters relating to Kashmir Shaivaism; lived towards the end and the beginning of the 11th century A. C.

Kshemarāja; pupil of above, continued the labours of his master; wrote the *Vimarshinī* on the *Shiva Sūtras, Commentaries* on the *Svachchhanda* and other Tantras besides other works.

Yogarāja, pupil of above and also of Abhinava with whom he must have begun his studies; author of a *Commentary* on Abhinava Gupta's *Paramārthasāra*.

Utpala Vaishṇava, author of the *Pradīpikā*, a commentary on the *Spanda-Kārikās*. He must have lived about this time as the authors he quotes are all earlier than this age but none later.

Rāma-Kaṇṭha (pupil of Utpalāchārya) author of the *Spanda-vivṛiti*.

The labours of the above were carried on by

Jayaratha

who lived at the end of the 12th century A. C.; and

Shivopādhyāya

who lived in the 18th century A. C.

As for the writings of the above the following list may be useful:—

1. Vasu Gupta — received inspirationally the *Shiva Sūtras.*
   wrote 1. *Spandāmṛita,* probably incorporated in the *Spanda Kārikās.*
   2. A *Commentary* on the *Bhagavad Gītā* called the *Vāsavī-Ṭīkā* of which the first six chapters are perhaps still to be found existing as incorporated in another Tīkā on the *Bha. Gītā* called *Lāsakī,* by Rājānaka Lasakāka, of which MSS. are available.

2. Kallaṭa[1] — wrote 1. *Spanda Kārikās*
   2. *Spanda Vṛitti* (or *Spanda Sarvasva*)
   3. *Tattvārtha-Chintāmaṇi* (lost)
   4. *Madhuvāhinī* (lost); both the above were Commentaries on the *Shiva Sūtras.*

3. Somānanda — wrote 1. *Shiva Dṛishṭi*
   2. A *Vṛitti* on the above.

---

1. Mukula, who wrote the *Alaṅkārodāharaṇa* and *Vivāhatattvānusmaraṇa* gives Kallaṭa as the name of his father. It is however doubtful if he was the son of our Kallaṭa.

4. **Utpalāchārya** wrote
1. *Pratyabhijñā Kārikās* or *Sūtras*.
2. *Vṛitti* on above; only incomplete Mss. available.
3. *Ṭīkā* on the same called *Vivṛiti* (lost)
4. *Stotrāvalī*
5. *Īshvara-Siddhi*
6. *Ajaḍapramātṛi-Siddhi*

5. **Rāma** wrote
1. *Spanda-Vivṛiti.*
2. Commentary on the *Mataṅga Tantra.* (?)
3. Commentary on the *Bh. Gītā* from the Shaiva point of view. (?)

6. **Utpala Vaishṇava** wrote *Spanda Pradīpikā* and other works referred to therein but now lost.

7. Abhinava Gupta wrote
1. *Mālinī- Vijaya- Vārttika* (lost)
2. *Parā-Triṁshikā-Vivaraṇa*
3. *Shiva-Dṛishṭyālochana* (lost)
4. *Pratyabhijñā- Vimarshinī* (Laghvī Vṛitti)
5. *Pratyabhijñā-Vivṛiti-Vimarshinī* (Bṛihatī Vṛitti)
6. *Tantrāloka*
7. *Tantrasāra*
8. *Paramārthasāra*

Besides numerous other works.

8. Bhāskara	wrote	*Shiva-Sūtra-Vārttika*
9. Kṣhemarāja	wrote	1. *Shiva-Sūtra-Vṛitti* (?) 2. *Shiva-Sūtra-Vimarshinī* 3. *Pratyabhijñā-Hṛidaya* (both Sūtras and commentary) 4. *Spanda-Sandoha.* 5. *Spanda- Nirṇaya* (incomplete). Besides Commentaries on several of the *Tantras.*
10. Yogarāja	wrote	*Commentary* on the *Paramārthasāra* of Abhinava Gupta.
11. Jayaratha	wrote	*Commentary* on the *Tantrāloka.*
12. Shivopādhyāya	wrote	*Commentary* on the *Vijñāna Bhairava Tantra.*

The following table showing the known facts as to the dates and mutual relation of the principal writers on Kashmir Shaivaism may also be appended here:—

Vasu Gupta

Bhaṭṭa-Nārāyaṇa (?)

Avantivarman = Kailaṭa = Somānanda = Muktākaṇa = Shiva Svāmin = Ānanda-Vardhana

Avantivarman: King of Kashmir. 855 to 883 A. C.

Kailaṭa: (pupil) c. 850 to 900 A. C.

Somānanda: (pupil?) c. 850 to 900 A. C.

Muktākaṇa: (descendant of Nārāyaṇa)

C. 815 to 900. (authors who flourished in the days of Avantivarman)

Pradyumna Bhaṭṭa (Mātuleya).
Prajñārjuna (son).
Mahādeva Bhaṭṭa (pupil).
Shrīkaṇṭha Bhaṭṭa (son).
Bhāskara (pupil).

Utpalāchārya (pupil) C. 900 to 950 A. C.
Lakṣhmaṇa Gupta (son and pupil) C. 950 to 1000.
Abhinava Gupta (pupil). C. 993 to 1015.
Kṣhemarāja (pupil).
Yogarāja (pupil).

Rāma Kaṇṭha (brother of Muktākaṇa and descendant of Narāyāṇa) Pupil of Utpalāchārya. C. 900 to 925.

Some Books in English on Kashmir Shaivism

Kaw, R.K. 1967. *The Doctrine of Recognition*. Hoshiarpur, India: Vishveshvaranand Institute.

Pandey, K.C. 1963. *Abhinavagupta: An Historical and Philosophical Study*. Varanasi-1, India: The Chowkhamba Sanskrit Series Office.

Pandit, B.N. 1977. *Aspects of Kashmir Saivism*. India: Utpal Publications.

Rastogi, Navjivan. 1979. *The Krama Tantricism of Kashmir*. Delhi, India: Motilal Banarsidass.

Rudrappa, J. 1969. *Kashmir Saivism*. University of Mysore, Mysore-6: Prasaranga.

Sharma, L. N. 1972. *Kashmir Shaivism*. Varanasi- India: Bharatiya Vidya Prakashan.

Singh, Jaideva, 1977. *Pratyabhijnahrdayam*. Delhi, India: Motilal Banarsidass.

Singh, Jaideva, 1979a. *Vijnanabhairava or Divine Consciousness*. Delhi, India: Motilal Banarsidass.

Singh, Jaideva, 1979b. *Siva Sutras: The Yoga of Supreme Identity*. Delhi, India: Motilal Banarsidass.

Singh, Jaideva, 1980. *Spanda-Karikas: The Divine Creative Pulsation*. Delhi, India: Motilal Banarsidass.

Index